INVESTING IN WRISTWATCHES

ROLEX

OSVALDO PATRIZZI
MARA CAPPELLETTI

ACC ART BOOKS

ROLEX
COSMOGRAPH
DAYTONA
UNITS PER
HOUR

CONTENTS

Preface: From Past to Future

by Osvaldo Patrizzi

Sometimes it's simply a 'spark' that ignites the interest that then becomes the passion of watch collecting. This passion may take many different forms and directions, from the elegant, simple dress watch to the complicated wristwatch. The complicated wristwatch fascinates us and takes us into the world of wonder, where minute-repeaters, perpetual calendars, chronographs, and such, mesmerise us with their precision, beauty, and functionality. One might, however, be drawn to timepieces that serve purely practical functions, such as the diver's, sports, military, or world time watches; these are found in so many different styles, forms, designs and materials that they fill the collector with enthusiasm. Some individuals approach collecting out of pure passion, while others decide to invest in their passion. The *Investing in Wristwatches* series of monographs is aimed at both types of collector – to inform them of the directions of the markets and the evolution of values from the beginning of this interest in the 1980s to the present day.

The worldwide exponential growth in this sector of horology has continued, despite the financial crises of the late '80s and early 2000s and new world records continue to be set in the auction world today. The goal of these books is to provide information based on official results, which translate to a real market basis. Some pieces that failed to sell at auction are included, as they are indicative of the market in that moment. Conversely, not all of the watches sold are present in the books, only those that seem to me to be the most representative for the purpose of the monograph; by omitting the occasional excesses, both in the high and the low prices achieved, it offers a truer picture. To provide a clearer understanding of prices reached during the sales, a list of the different currencies and their comparative values for that particular time period is included on p.318. An interesting point to keep in mind is that the watch purchased today may very well be the collector's watch of tomorrow.

Thanks to the collaboration with Sotheby's auction house, we can show the prices for a timepiece of the same reference from the '80s through to the most recently held auctions prior to the printing of each book. A comparative analysis of these results enables a better understanding of the evolution of the market value throughout the years, thanks to Sotheby's Worldwide allowing us access to their photographic archives and price results. We have chosen Sotheby's over other important auction houses, in order to maintain a stable average and linear progression of results over time. We would especially like to thank Daryn Schnipper, the Chairman of Sotheby's International Watch Division, and all her team.

To write these books I have asked Mara Cappelletti for her assistance. Mara is a journalist specialising in luxury products, as well as a jewellery and watch historian. We have collaborated on several watch books in the past, with great success. I would like to thank Mara for all her help – her assistance producing these latest books has greatly eased the process.

The first monograph of this series is dedicated to Rolex, one of the most prestigious brands in the world.

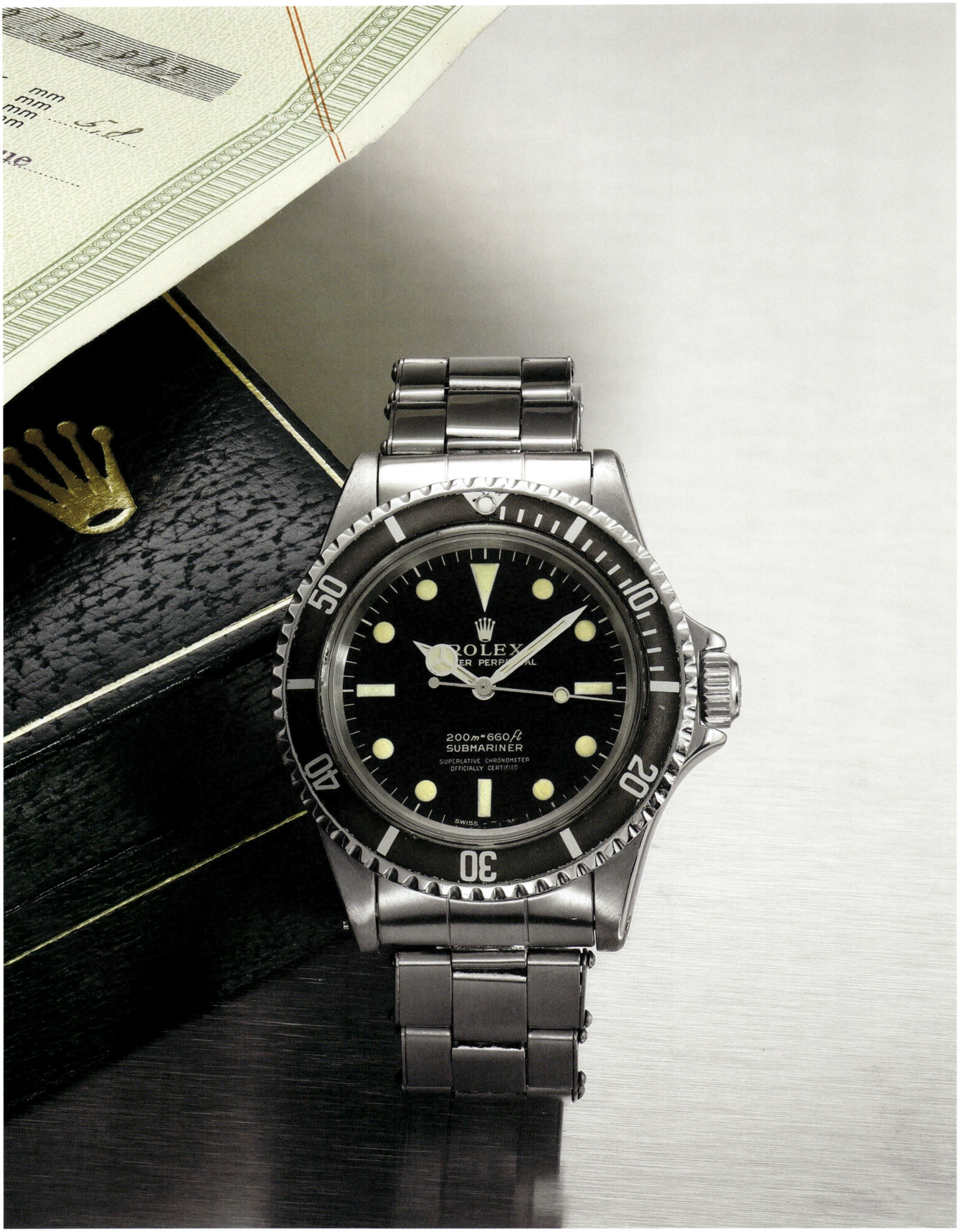
ROLEX
200m=660ft
SUBMARINER
SUPERLATIVE CHRONOMETER
OFFICIALLY CERTIFIED
50
10
40
20
30

The Wristwatch Comes of Age

by Daryn Schnipper

Sotheby's has been honoured to participate in the *Investing in Wristwatches* series of monographs. These exciting new books trace the development of the wristwatch market from its grass roots beginnings in the late 1970s until today. Offering a detailed perspective of the auction market through the most sought-after brands and their iconic models, these books illustrate market trends and developments over the last forty years.

As a collectable, the vintage wristwatch experienced a sudden growth in interest that caught many established watch collectors by surprise, and was met with great disdain – cries of 'It won't last!' and 'It's just a phase!' were common. Ironically, this echoed the same reaction from consumers when wristwatches were first introduced in the early 20th century. The idea of wearing a timepiece on one's wrist conjured up a decidedly feminine connotation, especially when compared to the much larger and more masculine pocket watch.

The advent of World War I rapidly changed this line of thought. The wristwatch became recognised for its practicality; after all, with a flick of the wrist, one could instantly know the time. In the trenches, this could mean the difference between life and death. Following the end of the war, the public accepted the more practical wristwatch into the mainstream consumer market. What followed was an explosion of design development and production, largely unabated until the Swiss watch quartz crisis decades later.

Fast forward to the 1980s and the collectors' market for vintage wristwatches was virtually a blank slate. There were no research resources or literature available. As a result, collectors had little knowledge about the production of vintage pieces. The majority of these early wristwatches had lain dusty, oxidised, and mostly forgotten at the bottom of drawers and in safety deposit boxes scattered around the globe. As the market solidified and prices rose, journalists took notice and covered the market with numerous articles. Indeed, collectors were coming together around the world, forming relationships and founding clubs all dedicated to a mutual passion for vintage wristwatches. The uptick in publicity raised awareness, leading to the unearthing of an abundance of vintage pieces. What ensued was the classic conundrum: what was collectable and what was not? Enthusiasts were learning on the go with no resources to guide them.

The market in the 1980s was one of organised chaos, as collectors fiercely debated which attributes made a wristwatch collectable: was its brand name or style, mechanical complexity or historical import of greatest significance? The answer to these questions changed repeatedly over the years. Eventually, collectors settled on brand as the key starting point.

Submariner 200m=660ft, Ref. 5512, which sold for CHF25,000 in 2014 (See p.192)

In 1983 Helmut Kahlert, Richard Mühe, and Gisbert Brunner published the first book about wristwatches, *Armbanduhren*, which detailed the history and development of the wristwatch. This new book provided a roadmap of sorts to the scope of timepiece production. Other books followed: in 1986, *I Signori Del*

Tempo by Giampiero Negretti and Franco Nencini and, in 1987, *Patek Philippe: Genève* by Martin Huber and Alan Banbery. While *I Signori Del Tempo* became a study in style and complications, collectors viewed the Patek Philippe book as a bible; this latter book undoubtedly contributed a great deal to the market's enduring success and was quickly followed by such seminal works as Osvaldo Patrizzi's *Orologi da Polso, Rolex*, published in 1992.

Detailed study of vintage wristwatches by the early enthusiasts gradually resulted in the dispersal of knowledge to a wider audience and collectors gained context, clarity, and confidence. Buyers armed with such knowledge made more informed decisions about the pieces they wished to add to their collections. By the late 1990s, the market had matured. To comprehend market growth, one need only study the trajectory of two models: Patek Philippe's Ref. 2499 and the Rolex 'Paul Newman' Daytona.

Patek Philippe produced the Ref. 2499 for 35 years from 1950 until 1985. It was the only perpetual calendar chronograph wristwatch made in series by the firm during this period. In 1983, a first series Ref. 2499 sold at Sotheby's for $16,500. Six years later, in 1989, a comparable Ref. 2499 first series sold at auction for $132,000. Today, the same first series Ref. 2499 easily surpasses the $1 million mark at auction.

Examining the ubiquitous Rolex 'Paul Newman' Daytona provides the second case study. Introduced to the market circa 1965, by the mid-1980s this model was fetching auction prices in the range of $1,000 and by the mid-1990s, its price had risen to $20,000. Today that same watch, depending on different dial characteristics, can sell from as low as $100,000 to as high as $1 million.

The rapidly developing vintage wristwatch market did not escape the attention of the Swiss houses. By 2000, the contemporary luxury market was flourishing and pushing technological boundaries. New investment was made in research and design and this was accompanied by brilliant marketing campaigns. New models appeared that clearly took inspiration from the past. Patek Philippe recreated the 1920s 'Gondolo', with both round and rectangular models. The firm paid further homage to the rectangular wristwatches of the 1940s and '50s, with vintage models such as the 'Eiffel Tower' (Ref. 2441) and the 'Manta Ray' (Ref. 2554) providing the inspiration for the new 'Pagoda' (Ref. 5500) and 'Millennium' (Ref. 5100) models, presented in 1997 and 2000, respectively. Patek Philippe also re-imagined another icon, the 'Calatrava', the epitome of classic style, in a more contemporary format. Audemars Piguet launched a new series of cushion-shaped minute repeating wristwatches called the 'John Schaeffer', after the original 1920s example they purchased at Sotheby's New York in 1989. In the 1970s, Gerald Genta designed the Audemars Piguet 'Royal Oak' and the Patek Philippe 'Nautilus.' These two models proved to be pillars for each brand and it was no surprise when, years later, each model was re-issued in a variety of new configurations.

Rolex, meanwhile, capitalised on the interest enjoyed by their vintage sports models, the Submariner, the GMT and the Daytona. Each model enjoyed subtle changes over the years. When the Daytona of the 1960s was redesigned and relaunched in 1988, demand quickly outstripped supply, creating a frenzy amongst fans.

The contemporary industry has evolved and grown astronomically in the last 20 years. Collectors have propelled the wristwatch into a dominant collecting category; one that far exceeds pocket watches in numbers, in global interest and in sales figures. It is interesting to note that exports of new Swiss wristwatches increased from CHF 15.9 billion in 2008 to CHF 20.5 billion in 2019 – according to figures from the Federation of the Swiss Watch Industry. In 2019, luxury watches were Switzerland's fifth largest export.

Today, the secondary market for contemporary luxury watches has eclipsed the vintage market in volume and value. It consists of both the established brands and independent makers, such as F.P. Journe, Richard Mille, Greubel Forsey, Urban Jürgensen and the English makers, Roger Smith and Charles Frodsham. The independents owe much to the celebrated modern British master watchmaker, the late George Daniels, who carved a path for today's independent makers. Daniels invented the first new watch escapement in 250 years; the Co-Axial, with its anti-frictional escapement, provided an efficient, modern mechanical alternative to quartz movements. Omega commercialised the Daniels Co-Axial in 1999. Daniels' body of work is small but revelatory. Most recently, in 2019, his Space Traveler I pocket watch sold for $4.5 million at Sotheby's London.

In the 2020s, with more than 100 hundred years of production, the wristwatch market is fully matured with the highest standards of quality and innovation. Iconic makers in the field have never rested on their laurels and continue to evolve and advance the limits of technology and artistic design. Their efforts have led the watch market to become one of the most popular collecting categories today.

Rolex, Building Icons

by Mara Cappelletti

Few companies can boast better brand awareness than Rolex. According to Forbes, Rolex is one of the top 100 most recognised and most powerful brands in the world. People, both inside and outside of the luxury watch world, recognise the name 'Rolex' and would associate it with success and status.

The brand owes its success to a number of reasons, including its ability to create a well-defined aesthetic, its high-impact marketing and communication campaigns and, in many ways, its role as the industry's standard-bearer. The significance of the Rolex name is primarily linked to the fact that the brand introduced innovative features quite early on that made the watch well-suited to everyday wear.

In 1905, Hans Wilsdorf and his brother-in-law, Alfred Davis, founded a watch company that officially took on the name Rolex in 1908. The name was chosen because it was easy to pronounce and could be written identically in European languages. In 1910, five years after its founding, Rolex produced its first watch to receive the Swiss Certificate for Chronometric Precision, thereby acknowledging the brand in the area of exact watchmaking.

Rolex went on to innovate constantly and several times brought new technologies to the market that eventually set standards for the whole industry: among them was the first waterproof wristwatch, the Rolex 'Oyster', in 1926. It was a turning point in the production of wristwatches. The wristwatch is taken for granted nowadays, as are features such as them being water-resistant, self-winding and accurate timekeepers. This was, however, seldom the case in the early 20th century, when pocket watches were still the norm and only a few people owned a wristwatch.

Wilsdorf strongly believed that wristwatches would become the standard in everyday life and concentrated on the development of technical features that would make this come true. The combination of waterproofing, as well as self-winding technology, made wristwatches undemanding timekeeping companions, thus leading to market growth. In 1931 a new innovation introduced by Rolex solved the problem of recharging. The Perpetual movement enabled the watch to self-wind depending only on the movements of the wrist to overcome inertia. Alongside these innovations in watchmaking during the first half of the 1900s, Rolex developed a reputation for reliability.

The adventure had begun and a long series of 'firsts' would mark the company's history. In 1945, the brand debuted the Datejust, the first self-winding wristwatch to display the date on the dial. In 1953, Rolex released the Submariner, the first diver's watch, waterproof to a depth of 100 metres. A year later, the brand introduced the GMT Master, which was the first watch to enable pilots to tell the time in multiple time zones simultaneously. In 1956, they unveiled the Day-Date – the first wristwatch to display the date and day of the week, in large letters in a dial aperture. The technical perfection of the mechanism and the use of precious metals also contributed to the success of Rolex's watches. In 1963, the famous Daytona Chronograph was launched. The Sea-Dweller, a high-tech watch introduced in 1967, was developed for deep-sea divers. Even watches that did not introduce mechanical innovations proved successful because of their reliability and appealing design.

During the '70s, a difficult decade for high-end automatic wristwatches due to the rise in popularity of the quartz movement, Rolex continued producing mechanical models. When the market for mechanical watches recovered in the 1980s and '90s, the company was well positioned to take a leadership role. The self-winding Daytona Chronograph was launched in 1988 and favourably received by the public. In 1992, Rolex unveiled the Yacht-Master, which helped sailors measure and anticipate the crucial countdown interval leading up to the start of a regatta or sailing race. In 2000, almost forty years after the Daytona debuted, Rolex launched the very first Daytona self-winding chronograph to boast an entirely in-house movement.

Among the launches of the new century is the Sky Dweller; released in 2012, this was the brand's first entirely new watch showcasing a dual time-zone, annual calendar and month indication. In recent years, the new releases have included the Daytona Ref. 116500, introduced in 2016 and featuring a bezel made of Cerachrom, Rolex's proprietary ceramic material that can withstand almost all wear and tear. In 2017, the company revamped the Sea-Dweller and, in 2020, new editions of the Submariner and the Oyster Perpetual series were introduced with new case sizes, new dial colours and new materials. The Rolex story continues...

The power of communication

The worlds of sport, aviation, motor racing and expeditions provided perfect real-life 'laboratories' for countless technical attributes of Rolex watches. For example, to mark the launch of their waterproof Oyster timepiece, Rolex sponsored an event that had global resonance. On 21 October 1927, the British swimmer Mercedes Gleitze, swam across the English Channel wearing an Oyster Precision watch. On her arrival, the watch was checked and declared to be 'working perfectly'. She was the first Englishwoman to manage the arduous swim, still a rare feat at the time, and she earned huge popular acclaim.

Wilsdorf celebrated the landmark event with a full-page advertisement on the front of London's *Daily Mail*, proclaiming the success of the first waterproof wristwatch, thus ensuring a wide public awareness of Rolex watches. Mercedes Gleitze effectively became the first Rolex endorser, her sporting achievement also demonstrating the new watch's qualities in action. Wilsdorf and his successors knew how to ensure their products became legendary. A Rolex watch also accompanied British driver Sir Malcolm Campbell on the nine times he set new land-speed records onboard his various *Bluebird* motor vehicles between 1924 and 1935.

Rolex watches have been to the top of the world and to the deepest recesses of the sea as well. The history of Rolex and exploration is one linked to some of the greatest adventures of the previous century. When Sir Edmund Hillary and Tenzing Norgay conquered Everest in 1953, thus proving that the climb to the peak of the world's highest mountain at 8,848 metres was not beyond man's reach, prototype Rolex Explorers were on their wrists.

In 1960, the bathyscaphe *Trieste*, piloted by Jacques Piccard and Lt. Don Walsh, carried an experimental Oyster watch, the Deep Sea Special, fixed to the vessel's exterior as it descended to a record depth of 10,916 metres in the Mariana Trench in the western Pacific Ocean, the deepest point in the oceans. The watch withstood the colossal pressure. Piccard and Walsh were the first people to reach the bottom of the ocean and it would be another 52 years before their achievement was matched by explorer and film-maker James Cameron in 2012. Cameron was also accompanied by a Rolex: the Deepsea Challenge, an experimental watch custom-made by Rolex to face the crushing pressure at this spectacular depth.

Over the years, Rolex has emphasised its presence in prestigious sports such as tennis and golf, motor racing, equestrian sports and sailing. Rolex has been the 'official timekeeper' at Wimbledon since 1978, at the U.S. Open since 1980, and for Formula One since 2013, clearly showing that Rolex represents the ideal instrument for sports and success. Athletes such as Phil Mickelson, Roger Federer, and Lindsay Vonn are proud Rolex ambassadors. Today, the Rolex crown, the logo introduced in 1925, serves as an iconic symbol associated with quality, innovation, and prestige.

Brand association

Over time, the *maison* has successfully associated its watches with remarkable people and the events connected to them. In addition to their work in the sporting world, Rolex has also made an impact in the areas of the arts and science. Rolex partners with the Academy of Motion Picture Arts & Sciences to support the art of filmmaking, and is a Founding Supporter of the new Academy Museum of Motion Pictures in Los Angeles. Today film directors Kathryn Bigelow, James Cameron, Alejandro Iñárritu and Martin Scorsese are brand ambassadors, though the liaison of Rolex with cinema started many years before. Sean Connery's 'James Bond' wore a Submariner; Steve McQueen wore (or so it seems) an Explorer II; Paul Newman, another devoted Rolex fan, wore his Daytona so often that the style – with its graphic black-and-white dial – has become known among collectors as a 'Newman Daytona'. In more recent times, Tom Cruise, Tom Hanks and Jennifer Aniston have been spotted wearing Rolex models.

Rolex also has long-term associations with the prestigious events and institutions that represent the highest level of achievement in music, such as the Vienna Philarmonic and Musikverein, the Salzburg Festival, the Teatro alla Scala in Milano, the Metropolitan Opera in New York, and the Royal Opera House in London.

The brand has also developed enduring partnerships with many of the world's top artists in architecture, dance, cinema, literature, music, theatre and visual arts, who always reach further to attain the pinnacle of their discipline. Both Eric Clapton and Placido Domingo are known to have sported Rolexes. The value of dreams and the importance of creativity are central to the maison and this has inspired the Rolex Mentor and Protégé Arts Initiative that enables a relation between master and apprentice in the above-mentioned artistic fields.

And last, but not least, Rolex annually funds organisations like the National Geographic to support aqua and nature conservation, wildlife protection as well as other environmental causes and projects.

The value of style

The basis for Rolex's success is its focus on select product franchises, each of which is characterised by extremely high product quality extending over the many years of its existence. Collections are maintained and continuously improved over the years with the introduction of upgrades and changes but without sudden design shifts or leaps. By doing this, all the Rolex models are kept relevant.

The company produces around 800,000 watches annually, and continually works on detail improvements. Larger cases, new movements, ceramic bezels and, now and again, a new colour. However, typical design features like the grooved bezel, 'Mercedes' hands, Cyclops magnifier and the Oyster bracelet are part of several different models and have rarely undergone changes, so a Datejust or a Submariner today looks very much like earlier models. This is why a Rolex may be the most instantly recognisable watch in the world.

In terms of product attributes, a Rolex watch features the finest materials in all its parts, such as the Oyster case and the Rolex self-winding movement, all of which have undergone rigorous testing by Rolex to ensure the highest quality control before the movements are sent to the independent Official Swiss Chronometer Testing Institute for chronometer certification.

In the Rolex branding policy, every detail is important. Rolex prohibits the sale of new watches online and strictly selects eligible outlets where prospective customers can experience and purchase the *maison*'s timepieces. Company and product reputation contribute to maintaining and sustaining a Rolex's value. Rolex watches are perceived as having a higher resale value than other luxury goods, making a Rolex a sure investment for collectors. While many items, such as cars, drop in value immediately upon purchase, this is less true for Rolex – an attractive proposition for any customer, whether they wear the watch or simply speculate financially on the watch's value.

The economic dynamics of previously owned Rolex watches are sustained by the record prices often attained at auction. There are hundreds of examples of auctioning success with Rolex watches over the last several decades. In some cases, the results have been astonishingly high. The value of these iconic watches does not merely endure over time but grows constantly, as attested to by the consistently positive sales results accrued over the years. However, the prices attracted by these watches at auction cannot simply be explained on the basis of their fine craftmanship, or the fact that they once belonged to celebrities; what increases their value is the legend, the desire and an aura of exceptionality that Rolex has always been very good at nurturing.

Highlights on Rolex

By Daryn Schnipper

Rolex is instantly one of the most recognisable global brands. While initially one might think that Rolex has earned its reputation through production numbers, I believe it has to do with the brand's single-minded focus on making a watch for a specific purpose. This strategy brilliantly identified Rolex watches as Tool or Sports watches intended for those living a rugged lifestyle. From the mountain climber, deep-sea diver, aeroplane pilot, the yachtsman, the race car driver, to even the scientist working in high magnetic fields, Rolex has been able to produce a model with attributes specifically related to these fields, thus building an international group of avid collectors.

Rolex has a unique attribute in their famous Ambassadors, who have inspired discerning buyers through the decades to wear a Rolex. From Sir Edmund Hillary wearing his Rolex while summitting Mt. Everest, to Jacques Cousteau using his Rolex in the depths of the ocean floor, to the Pan Am pilots who used theirs while travelling on the first transatlantic flights, Rolex has been able to link its identity to these famous explorers, thus helping it build international acclaim. Arguably the most famous of all is Paul Newman's Daytona, his personal watch worn when he starred in the movie *Winning*.

Of the numerous notable Ambassadors, some have stood the test of time as true icons. The 20th century produced some legends such as Edmund Hillary's Sherpa, Tensing Norgay, whose Rolex Ref. 3372 with the cloisonné enamel map of India commemorating the nation's independence from England captured collectors' collective imaginations. It would be remiss not to mention Sean Connery and Roger Moore, whose portrayals of James Bond wearing the Submariner left indelible marks on the history of Rolex in cinema. Rolex Ambassadors spanned genres, from cultural superstars Steve McQueen and opera singer Placido Domingo to golfers Phil Mickelson, Tiger Woods and Jack Nicklaus. The success of these men in their professions has helped cement Rolex as an icon in the cultural zeitgeist for decades.

A never-ending passion

The most sought-after references are without a doubt the Daytona, the Submariner, the GMT, the Explorer, and the Day-Date. Rather than staying stagnant, these models have evolved over the decades with myriad variations. Each time the firm announces a new upgrade or design deviation, the furore only grows as collectors clamour to acquire the new model.

However, if we take the long view of the second-hand market, we can see that customer preferences have changed through the years. When collectors initially gained an interest in wristwatches in the late 1970s, the early Rolex models from the 1920s to 1950s were very popular. Demand continued into the 1980s and mid-'90s.

During these early years of wristwatch collecting, wristwatch aficionados were captivated by early Rolex time-only models, such as cushion- and octagonal-shaped cases with enamel dials, dubbed 'Oyster' models. Rolex buyers were also interested in the Prince, a rectangular watch made in the 1940s and the bubble back, so-called due to its domed-shaped case back, which housed the firm's patented self-winding rotor. As scholarship grew in the 1990s, trends expanded to include all of Rolex's sport models, with great attention paid to the GMT, the Submariner, the Daytona and the Explorer, which are still highly popular today.

Currently, the Rolex Daytona fetches by far the most outstanding results. In 2020, in the midst of the global pandemic, Sotheby's sold two Rolex Daytonas within a two-week time period, each for record prices. The first was a unique Rolex Daytona in platinum with a hardstone lapis lazuli dial, Ref. 16516, which sparked worldwide excitement leading to a record selling price of HK$ 25.4 million ($3.3 million). Two weeks later, we sold a Rolex Ref. 6264 in 18k gold with a JPS Paul Newman dial for £1.2 million ($1.5 million).

In a story I particularly love, we sold a 'Paul Newman' Daytona Ref. 6239 in 2018. It came straight from the original owner, who had received the watch as a 25th wedding anniversary present, complete with the receipt for original purchase price of £134 in 1975. This 'Paul Newman' had an unusual dial that we call Tropical, which is when the colour of the subsidiary dial plates transitions from black to a toffee brown. We sold this watch in Geneva, on behalf of an astonished seller, who looked on as his watch sold for the life-changing sum of CHF950,000 (see p.64).

For me, probably the most memorable Rolex sale at Sotheby's took place in May of 2002 in Hong Kong. The single owner sale, entitled 'Rolex Sporting Time', consisted of solely Rolex watches. The sale featured over 300 lots and included pieces from the 1920s to the '90s. It presented collectors with a unique opportunity not only to buy exclusive examples of the most sought-after Rolexes, but also to see the historic evolution of the pieces they knew and loved. So important was the sale, collectors travelled from around the globe to Hong Kong and, to our utter astonishment, the exhibition was so popular we had queues of people out through the door waiting to get in. In fact, when we offered priority clients immediate entrance, they declined because they enjoyed the communal enthusiasm of waiting in line with their fellow Rolex connoisseurs. Needless to say, the sale was a tremendous success. The sale commanded a premium at the time; but how wonderful it would be to hold that sale again today!

I think the greatest aspect of the watch as a collectible is the fact that you can own something tangible that you can wear and enjoy. The emotional connection a collector has with a watch they can wear and attribute memories to cannot be replaced by stocks and bonds. That said, the most important aspect of buying watches for investment is that you like what you buy even if you do not intend to wear it.

A Special Relationship

by Osvaldo Patrizzi

Since the beginning of my activity as owner and director of an auction house, the then Geneva-based Galerie Genevoise d'Horlogerie Ancienne, which I founded together with Gabriel Tortella in 1974, I have traded exclusively in horology. In April 1981, I held the first worldwide auction dedicated entirely and exclusively to wristwatches – and it turned out to be quite a success.

A novelty in the auction market, I also introduced innovative catalogues that (in addition to the detailed information on the watches themselves) included the historical background and biographies of renowned owners, thereby tracing a history of the *maisons* through their most prestigious and illustrious customers over two centuries. By choosing a single watchmaker or manufacturer, through a thematic sale, it was possible to tell its story, thus imparting a deeper knowledge of the spirit and soul of a brand, enabling the collector to purchase not only a timepiece, but a piece of history. The provenance of a timepiece can have a significant impact on the emotional aspect and, consequently, on the price that a buyer is willing to pay for it. Since the very beginning, Rolex proved to be central to the auction market as the brand has always attracted many collectors.

A turning point in luxury wristwatch auctions was the naming of models rather than using the reference number, an innovation that I introduced back in the early Nineties, to create a 'sexy' appeal linked to a legendary figure. One of the early examples of this regards a Rolex watch. I came up with the idea of calling the Rolex Daytona reference 6239 by the name 'Paul Newman' after seeing a photograph of the American actor wearing that model. It was a Rolex Cosmograph with an unusual two-tone dial, different from the other classic dials. A gift to the actor from his wife Joanne Woodward, it was a watch that he wore often, including on the set of the film *Winning* – it even appeared on the film poster. My idea came to fruition at an auction in Basel on 21 April 1990 when I launched the so-called 'Paul Newman' and the model sold with such enthusiasm that the legend of the iconic 'Daytona Paul Newman' was born. By associating such a beloved actor with the values of the Rolex brand, the value of the watch was greatly increased and it became hugely sought after. Another example of this new, emotional type of communication was the idea of calling references 4767, 6036 and 6236 by the name of the famous Olympic ski champion, Jean-Claude Killy, a great fan of Rolex watches who loved to wear this triple-date chronograph model. This reference, which went to auction in Geneva in April 1997, was also greatly appreciated by the collectors and became part of the history of collecting.

Choosing to replace reference numbers with names was certainly a winning move in facilitating their identification. It allows one to go beyond just the technical and stylistic characteristics; the myth, the desire, and the concept of exceptionality takes over. It took several years, but other auction houses eventually followed suit.

I had realised why certain Rolex Daytona chronograph dials tend to change colour over time. The colour change is due to the fact that the company used a very thin organic varnish, called Zapon, to protect the dial; however, with time and ultra-violet light, the dial oxidises. This reaction often creates interesting shades of colour, making each watch a unique piece.

One of the best examples of these watches made interesting by oxidation is Ref. 16520. Introduced at the end of 1993, it features a black dial with three silver subsidiary dials; it tends, gradually, to become a dark brown – the 'Patrizzi dial' as I was glad to discover it had been named by collectors. Therefore, my relationship with Rolex has become a very personal one.

Rarity increases value

Of course, limited editions add value to each item. In 1928, Rolex introduced the Prince model (and its counterpart, the Princess), available in various sizes and with various combinations of different metals. With its Art Deco look, this model was to become the first Rolex icon. Following this design period, Rolex discovered its true calling. Among Rolex's most acclaimed limited-edition watches are the early chronographs, which were marketed between the 1930s and '50s. Designed specifically as functional objects, they would have been worn by engineers, sportsmen and officers as a work tool. Requiring a high degree of accuracy and reliability, they were manufactured only in small numbers, which is what makes them all the more valuable today.

In 2006, the Mondani Collection of 309 Rolex Wristwatches realised the astounding total of CHF 11,037,278. Several world records were set during this sale, most significantly by Ref. 4113. Born as a military watch, this split-second chronograph sold for CHF 738,500, the highest price ever attained by a Rolex watch at that time.

In 1947, Rolex introduced a model with triple date and chronograph, which takes its name from the complete calendar (dato) and the three subsidiary chronograph dials known as 'compax'. The so-called 'Dato Compax' was born. In 1950, Rolex, which until then had produced few complicated watches, started developing some intricate moonphase mechanisms. Of these moonphase watches (Refs. 8171 and 6062), 350 were manufactured in yellow gold, as well as 50 in pink gold and with a very limited number in stainless steel. On account of their rarity, these pieces are highly sought after by collectors.

Sporty and classy

Created in 1953, the Submariner was officially launched at the 1954 Basel Watch Fair. The bezel was designed in such a way that it could only move anti-clockwise to prevent divers from making mistakes when recording their time underwater. The very first innovation began with Ref. 6204, featuring a graphic black dial punctuated by an inverted triangle at 12 o'clock, a black, gilt-finish rotating bezel, luminous baton indices at 3, 6 and 9, and dot indices for the remaining hours. All of these features offered superior legibility in the ocean's depths.

In the Submariner's early years, Rolex was almost constantly tweaking the design, so examples can be found with a number of subtle variations, such as a 'clean dial' without the Submariner demarcation, alternate sizing of the words 'Oyster Perpetual', and so on.

The submariner was to become sought-after thanks to its association with a certain secret agent. Beginning with Sean Connery in *Dr. No*, James Bond wore a Submariner 6538 in his first four films, bringing life to the watch's adventurous allure. Subsequent 007s would sport various Submariners up to *License to Kill* in 1989. One 6538, with a NATO strap and no bezel, set the record price for a Submariner, fetching $1,068,500 in 2018.

Today, the Submariner boasts a water pressure endurance of 300 metres and innovations such as a virtually indestructible Cerachrom bezel and an adjustable Glidelock bracelet that enables divers to wear it over their wetsuits.

Created for pilots, made for success

Back in the 1950s, commercial airlines had opened up a whole new world of exploration. Pan Am, the first airline to provide intercontinental flights without a stopover, challenged Rolex to create a watch equipped to display two time zones – for both the departure city and destination – simultaneously.

Rolex's response was the GMT-Master, which debuted in 1954. In addition to the standard hours, minutes and seconds hands, the GMT-Master displays the second time zone through a fourth 24-hour hand. This is bolstered by the GMT-Master's distinctive two-tone rotating bezel with 24-hour numerals; pilots could set the fourth hand to Greenwich Mean Time (the standard from which all time zones are measured) and rotate the bezel accordingly. The bezel's two colours correspond to daytime (red) or night time (blue) hours. While the GMT-Master was created to serve professional pilots, its function was equally attractive to the burgeoning class of frequent flyers and so it soon became the watch of the jet-set elite.

The GMT-Master's enduring appeal has spawned numerous variations since it was first introduced. The original blue and red bezel is known as the 'Pepsi' among collectors; later variations include the red and black 'Coke', brown and gold 'Root Beer' (Ref. 16753); and the blue and black 'Batman'. Ref. 1675, introduced in 1959 and produced until 1980, is one of the most highly sought-after GMT-Master models amongst collectors. In 1983, Rolex introduced the GMT-Master II. Aesthetically, the two models are nearly identical; the real difference is the powerful mechanism ticking away inside the GMT-Master II.

Ever evolving towards greater precision, Rolex ceased production of the GMT-Master in 1999 to focus on the technologically advanced GMT-Master II. Eventually, the aluminium bezel inserts were replaced with virtually indestructible ceramic in several of the iconic colour combinations. For the most part, however, this classic has retained all the trappings that made it part of the modern watch canon. Whether contemporary or vintage, the GMT-Master's jet-set allure is still an international emblem of the high (flying) life.

Icon of icons

Among the brand's many coveted models, the Daytona is the absolute icon. It is not one of the most complicated or intricate timepieces – it didn't introduce any technical breakthroughs or set any records – yet it is an undeniable object of desire, immediately recognisable throughout the world. However, when it was introduced on the market, the model did not immediately find success. In the early 1960s, classic-looking, ultra-thin watches were still in vogue, and the Cosmograph, as it was originally called, was considered bulky.

The brand had introduced its first chronographs in the 1930s and continued producing them throughout the 1940s and '50s. When the Daytona Speedway opened in 1959, it was one of the world's greatest venues for motorsports. In 1962, Rolex became Daytona's official timekeeper – a distinction the brand holds to this day. A year later, bolstered by the Daytona partnership, Rolex's remastered chronograph premiered. Although it was nicknamed the 'Daytona' within the company, Ref. 6239 was known as the Cosmograph (taken from a previous model dating from the 1950s, Ref. 6062). The name 'Daytona' wouldn't appear on the dial until 1964.

Over the next 25 years, Rolex perfected and transformed this manual chronograph, always striving to enhance the durability, appearance and precision of the watch. The manual Daytona evolved over six references until it was replaced in 1988 with the automatic Daytona. Today, these ultra-rare models are some of the most coveted, and most valuable watches on the pre-owned and collector's market.

It was in the late 1960s that Ref. 6239 attracted a celebrity devotee. Paul Newman wasn't just an actor, he was also an outstandingly successful racecar driver. His Daytona watch accompanied him on his races. It seemed so obvious to me that as this watch was associated with Paul Newman, it was logical to name it after him.

Paul Newman with his wife, actress Joanne Woodward, during a break in filming
© KEYSTONE Pictures USA / Alamy Stock Photo

ROLEX

PRINCE

Geneva, 16 November, 2004

Rectangular two-colour gold duo-dial wristwatch with flared sides
Ref. 971
Prince
*c.*1930

CHF 7,000 – 9,000
US$ 5,600 – 7,200

SOLD CHF 7,800

Originally released to the market in 1928, the Rolex Prince, or 'Doctor's Watch', was an unbelievably accurate wristwatch. Often fitted with a chronometer movement, the model featured a subsidiary seconds register below the hours and minutes section of the dial, enabling a doctor to time pulses and respiration rates, hence its moniker. Rolex capitalised on this concept during the period, marketing the watch to professionals in the medical sector. This reference 971 features a two-tone gold case.

1 New York, 15 June, 1999

Rare rectangular platinum wristwatch
Ref. 1490
Prince
*c.*1930

US$ 35,000 – 40,000

SOLD US$ 23,500

2 New York, 15 June, 1999

Rectangular gold jump-hour wristwatch with bracelet
Ref. 1490
Prince
*c.*1930

US$ 7,000 – 9,000

SOLD US$ 12,650

3 New York, 15 June, 1999

Rare rectangular two-tone gold duo-dial wristwatch
Ref. 1490
Prince
*c.*1930

US$ 12,000 – 15,000

SOLD US$ 18,000

Two models were introduced during the late 1920s: the more subdued rectangular 'doctor's watch', Ref. 1343, and the flared-sided Brancard, Ref. 1490. In 1930, Rolex introduced the platinum 'Brancard', at the time it was the most expensive watch that Rolex offered for sale.

1

2

3

1 Hong Kong, 27 April, 2004

Fine rectangular gold duo-dial wristwatch with flared sides and curved back
Ref. 1490
Prince Brancard
c.1930

HK$ 50,000 – 70,000
US$ 6,500 – 9,000

SOLD HK$ 69,600

2 Hong Kong, 27 April, 2004

Rare rectangular gold quarter-century wristwatch with duo dial and flared sides
Ref. 1490
Prince Brancard
c.1944

HK$ 40,000 – 55,000
US$ 5,200 – 7,100

SOLD HK$ 69,600

3 Geneva, 16 November, 2004

Rectangular gold duo-dial wristwatch with flared sides
Ref. 1490
Prince
c.1937

CHF 5,500 – 6,500
US$ 4,400 – 5,200

SOLD CHF 6,000

4 London, 17 July, 2019

Rectangular stainless-steel wristwatch
Retailed by Bucherer
Ref. 1490 MVT 74'236
Case 038'525
Prince
c.1937

£ 3,000 – 5,000

SOLD £ 5,000

1

2

3

4

1 Geneva, 16 November, 2004

Rectangular gold duo-dial wristwatch
Ref. 1527
Prince, Railway
*c.*1935

CHF 8,000 – 12,000
US$ 6,400 – 9,600

SOLD CHF 11,400

In 1935, Rolex launched a variation to its classic rectangular model, the Railway Prince, Ref. 1527.

One of the first Prince models to be produced in steel, the Railway proved to be rather unpopular and was produced in lower numbers than other models. Consequently, fewer examples are seen today and it is now considered rarer and, thus, more collectible.

Production of Ref. 1491 started in the 1930s and it features the jump hour complication.

2 Geneva, 16 November, 2004

Rare rectangular two-colour gold jump-hour wristwatch with duo dial and flared sides
Ref. 1491
Prince
*c.*1930

CHF 10,000 – 15,000
US$ 8,000 – 11,900

SOLD CHF 20,400

1

2

New York, 15 June, 1999

Rare rectangular platinum
jump-hour wristwatch
with duo dial
Ref. 1491
Prince
c.1935

US$ 20,000 – 25,000

SOLD US$ 18,000

Geneva, 17 May, 2005

Rare rectangular stainless-steel
jump-hour wristwatch with
flared sides
Ref. 1491HS
Prince, Heures Sautantes
c.1935

CHF 24,000 – 28,000
US$ 15,500 – 18,100

SOLD CHF 28,800

Geneva, 14 May, 2014

Rectangular yellow-gold
wristwatch with black dial
Ref. 2771
Case 39048
Prince
c.1952

CHF 6,000 – 8,000
US$ 6,900 – 9,100

SOLD CHF 22,500

The Prince was one of the most accurate wristwatches made up to the 1930s. The accuracy of the watch comes from the high-quality balance wheel, which uses solid gold screws to add extra weight, thus giving the wheel far more momentum. The high-quality finishing to the escapement, even the wheels, ensures the accuracy of the Prince movement. Production of Ref. 2771 started mid 1930s and had ended by the mid 1950s.

Geneva, 13 May, 2003

Rare gold hunting-cased wristwatch with duo dial
Ref. 1879
Prince, Sporting Prince
*c.*1934

CHF 20,000 – 30,000
US$ 15,000 – 20,000

SOLD CHF 31,200

The Prince, with winding and balance wheel placed on two different levels, allows for a larger balance and more precision. Many different versions were made including the Sporting Prince. Prior to the introduction of shock-resistant balances, it had been inadvisable to play a sport while wearing a watch.

TELEMETRE 1Km
ROLEX
ANTI-MAGNETIQUE

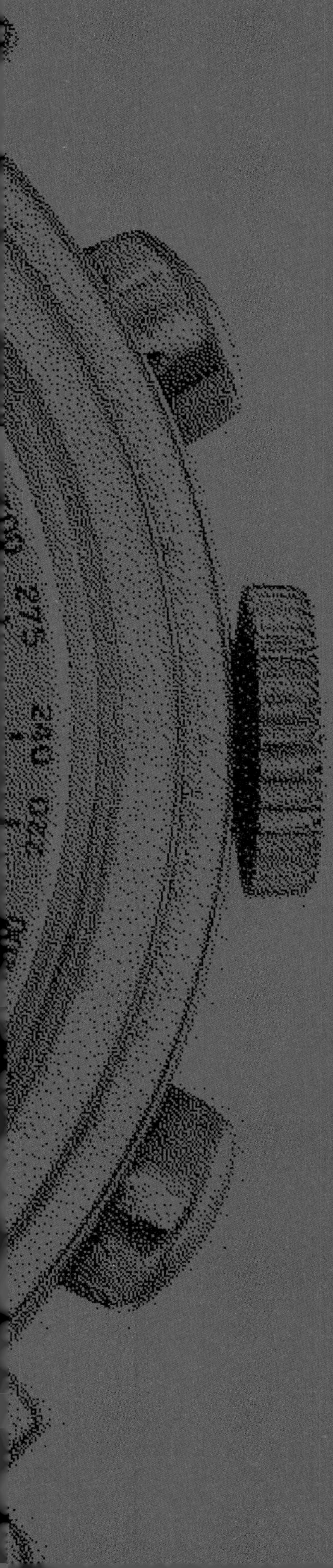

CHRONOGRAPH

Geneva, 16 May, 2007

Rare cushion-form silver chronograph wristwatch with registers
Ref. 2022
Chronograph
*c.*1929

CHF 40,000 – 50,000
US$ 33,100 – 41,400

SOLD CHF 93,600

Ref. 2022 is an important model in the development of the Rolex chronograph. It is one of the first chronographs made by the company, one of the very few single-button models and one of the only cushion-form chronographs Rolex has manufactured. Additionally, it is highly unusual to find a Rolex chronograph in a silver case; interestingly, an advertisement from the 1930s displayed the model as available in either steel or gold, suggesting that silver was not a standard metal used in the production of this reference.

New York, 5 December, 2005

Rare cushion-form single-button gold chronograph wristwatch with register
Ref. 2057
'Anti-magnetique'
Chronograph
c.1930

US$ 20,000 – 30,000

SOLD US$ 22,800

Geneva, 17 May, 2005

Exceptionally rare single-button stainless-steel fly-back chronograph with two-tone dial
Ref. 3346
Chronograph 'Centregraph'
*c.*1935

CHF 70,000 – 90,000
US$ 45,100 – 58,000

NOT SOLD

Introduced around the mid 1930s, Ref. 3346 (also known as 'Centregraph') is an exceptionally rare Rolex model; fewer than 50 examples are believed to have been produced. With a fly-back chronograph, the movement incorporates a mechanism – via a pusher in the case side – to reset the central seconds hand, at which point counting recommences.

1 Geneva, 10 November, 2015

Rare yellow-gold chronograph wristwatch with tachymeter
Ref. 2508
Case 46876
Chronograph
c.1947

CHF 10,000 – 12,000
US$ 10,300 – 12,300

SOLD CHF 62,500

2 Geneva, 12 November, 2019

Stainless-steel chronograph wristwatch
Ref. 2508
Case 037'620
Chronograph
c.1937

CHF 100,000 – 200,000
US$ 101,000 – 202,000

NOT SOLD

Rolex first introduced Ref. 2508 in the mid-1930s, representing the very beginning of their chronograph lineage. This reference was the first to feature two pushers to operate the chronograph and the two subsidiary dials, one of which displays the running seconds and the other features a 30-minute register. Production continued into the late 1940s.

1

2

1 Geneva, 14 May, 2017

Anti-magnetic stainless-steel chronograph wristwatch with tachymeter, telemeter and register
Ref. 2917
Case 031672
Chronograph
c.1937

CHF 10,000 – 15,000
US$ 10,200 – 15,300

SOLD CHF 10,000

2 Geneva, 15 November, 2009

Very rare stainless-steel chronograph wristwatch with register
Ref. 2918
Chronograph
c.1937

CHF 30,000 – 50,000
US$ 29,100 – 48,500

SOLD CHF 37,500

Since the 1930s, watchmakers have been concerned with addressing the problem of magnetism and frequently used soft iron-dust covers and the addition of anti-magnetic parts, often made out of gold, to counter the effects of magnetism. The reference 2918 was produced in small numbers in the mid 1930s and only in stainless steel. It is particularly notable for its unusual flexible lugs.

These models feature the word 'antimagnetic' if produced for English-speaking markets or 'anti-magnetique' if made for French-speaking countries.

1

2

Geneva, 16 November, 2008

Rare small anti-magnetic pink-gold chronograph wristwatch with tachymeter scale
Ref. 3055
Chronograph 'Piccolino'
c.1945

CHF 23,000 – 28,000
US$ 20,600 – 25,100

NOT SOLD

Ref. 3055 is one of the smallest chronograph wristwatches in the world. The reference was first produced in the 1930s with olive-shaped pushers and reintroduced during the 1950s with square chronograph pushers. When first launched by Rolex, it was advertised as the world's smallest chronograph.

Geneva, 16 November, 2008

Anti-magnetic stainless-steel
chronograph wristwatch
with register, tachymeter, telemeter
and two-tone dial
Retailed by Giudici, Milano
Ref. 3233
Chronograph
c.1940

CHF 25,000 – 35,000
US$ 22,400 – 31,400

SOLD CHF 27,500

Ref. 3233 was launched in 1938 and was available until around 1941. A noteworthy point to mention is the lugs, which are fixed inside the case and so cannot be removed. The watch features a silvered dial, baton and Arabic numerals, telemeter and tachymeter scales, circular case and hidden lugs.

Geneva, 16 May, 2006

Very rare, large gold chronograph wristwatch with pink dial and faceted lugs
Retailed by Astrua
Ref. 3335
Chronograph
*c.*1940

CHF 25,000 – 35,000
US$ 19,300 – 27,000

SOLD CHF 72,000

The rare Ref. 3335 was the first Rolex chronograph produced with 30-minute and 12-hour registers. It was produced for a period of one year only, between 1939 and 1940. Only 250 pieces were made, variously with pink, yellow-gold and stainless-steel cases.

New York, 5 December, 2005

Rare steel chronograph
wristwatch with register
and two-tone dial
Ref. 3484
Chronograph 'Anti-Magnetic'
c.1940

US$ 10,000 – 15,000

SOLD US$ 12,000

Ref. 3484 was in production from 1937 to 1948 and was cased either in stainless steel or gold. Being anti-magnetic, it features a precision regulator, two-tone silvered dial with Roman and baton indexes, an inner ring calibrated for telemeter scale and an outer ring calibrated for tachymeter scale, two engine-turned subsidiary dials indicating constant seconds and 30-minute register, blued steel hands, large circular case with downturned lugs, rectangular chronograph pushers in the band, and snap back.

Geneva, 16 May, 2006

Exceptional steel chronograph wristwatch with register, tachymeter and telemeter
Ref. 3525
Oyster
Chronograph
*c.*1940

CHF 25,000 – 35,000
US$ 19,300 – 27,000

SOLD CHF 132,000

Ref. 3525 was one of Rolex's earliest Oyster-cased chronographs and remains amongst the most popular with collectors. Production of this reference seems to have begun either at the very end of the 1930s or beginning of the 1940s.

This model is commonly known as the 'monoblock' chronograph, a name that comes from that fact that the bezel and top are one piece, in contrast to the later 'Pre-Daytona' in which these parts are separate.

A limited number of Ref. 3525s are the so-called 'Prisoner of War' watches, which were purchased by Allied prisoners of war in Nazi German camps during WWII. These watches would be brought to the prison camps by the Red Cross and given to the officers for free, with the provision that they would pay for them in instalments at the end of the war.

Geneva, 16 May, 2007

Stainless-steel chronograph
wristwatch with register, tachymeter
and telemeter
Ref. 3525
Oyster
Chronograph
*c.*1940

CHF 12,000 – 18,000
US$ 10,000 – 14,900

SOLD CHF 24,000

New York, 13 June, 2007

Stainless-steel chronograph
wristwatch with register,
tachymeter and telemeter
Ref. 3525
Chronograph 'Anti-Magnetic'
'Monoblock'
*c.*1945

US$ 45,000 – 55,000

SOLD US$ 57,000

Geneva, 11 May, 2013

Stainless-steel chronograph wristwatch with register, expansible bracelet and pulsometer scale
Ref. 3525
Case 186058 Monobloсco Chronograph
c.1940

CHF 40,000 – 60,000
US$ 42,400 – 64,000

SOLD CHF 47,500

Geneva, 14 May, 2014

Pink-gold chronograph wristwatch with register, tachymeter and telemeter
Retailed by Verga
Ref. 3525
Chronograph 'Anti-Magnetic'
c.1945

CHF 70,000 – 100,000
US$ 79,500 – 114,000

SOLD CHF 185,000

Geneva, 12 November, 2013

Very rare stainless-steel chronograph wristwatch with registers, telemeter and tachymeter
Ref. 3666
Case 041928
Chronograph 'Anti-Magnetic'
c.1940

CHF 25,000 – 35,000
US$ 27,000 – 37,800

SOLD CHF 161,000

Very few Ref. 3666 Rolex chronographs are known to the market. This is an exquisite example of the reference with its perfectly aged stainless-steel case and stunning pink dial, which features a blue telemeter scale.

Geneva, 16 May, 2007

Pink-gold chronograph wristwatch
with registers and tachymeter
Retailed by Giudici
Ref. 3695
c.1940

CHF 15,000 – 20,000
US$ 12,500 – 16,600

SOLD CHF 69,600

Introduced in 1940, this reference was developed for an extremely short amount of time and it is one of the rarest chronographs produced by Rolex.

Geneva, 10 November, 2015

Rare yellow-gold chronograph wristwatch with champagne dial, registers and unusual lugs
Ref. 3835
Case 57484
Chronograph
*c.*1940

CHF 35,000 – 45,000
US$ 35,800 – 46,000

NOT SOLD

Manufactured during the 1940s, it is believed that only a very small number of these non-Oyster anti-magnetic Ref. 3835s were ever made. The yellow-gold models are apparently rarer than the pink-gold models.

1 Geneva, 17 May, 2004

Very rare stainless-steel chronograph wristwatch with register and pulsation dial
Ref. 4048
Oyster
Chronograph
*c.*1940

CHF 60,000 – 80,000
US$ 38,600 – 51,500

NOT SOLD

The design of Ref. 4048 demonstrates its position at a turning point in the aesthetic of Rolex chronographs. Various examples within the reference bear small subsidiary dials that were favoured on earlier chronographs, while others have large subsidiary dials, the look that is seen in chronographs to this day. During the 1940s, some chronographs were still made with square pushers, while others, such as Ref. 4048, utilised the more modern round chronograph pushers.

2 New York, 17 October, 2008

Rare stainless-steel chronograph wristwatch with register, tachymeter and telemeter
Ref. 4048
Chronograph 'Monobloc'
*c.*1940

US$ 55,000 – 75,000

SOLD US$ 74,500

1 Although the pulsometer was commonly used on pocket watches from the late 19th century, it is very unusual to find such a scale on wristwatch chronographs (manufacturers preferred using tachymeter and telemetric scales). Rolex does not seem to have used the pulsometer scale with any regularity. Very few examples of Ref. 4048 are known to exist with a pulsation dial and this particular example is notable for its exceptional condition.

New York, 8 June, 2006

Rare stainless-steel chronograph wristwatch with register, telemeter, tachymeter and bracelet
Ref. 4500
Oyster
Chronograph 'Anti-Magnetique'
c.1946

US$ 16,000 – 18,000

NOT SOLD

London, 14 July, 2011

18k yellow-gold chronograph wristwatch with register, tachymeter and bracelet
Ref. 4500
Oyster 'Monobloc'
Chronograph 'Anti-Magnetic'
c.1947

£ 15,000 – 20,000
€ 17,000 – 22,700
US$ 24,500 – 32,700

SOLD £ 21,250

New York, 24 May, 2018

Rare anti-magnetic yellow-gold chronograph wristwatch with pulsation dial and bracelet
Ref. 4500
Case 480857 'Monobloc'
Chronograph
c.1946

US$ 50,000 – 100,000
€ 40,700 – 81,500
HK$ 393,000 – 785,000

SOLD US$ 62,500

Geneva, 14 May, 2014

Rare pink-gold chronograph wristwatch with register, tachymeter and telemeter
Ref. 4500
Case 480907
Chronograph 'Anti-Magnetique'
c.1946

CHF 50,000 – 80,000
US$ 57,000 – 91,000

SOLD CHF 125,000

Ref. 4500 was launched in the 1940s and was only produced for a short period of time. It was available in yellow gold, pink gold, stainless steel as well as stainless steel with gold.

It is one of the very few Oyster chronograph models to feature only two subsidiary dials: constant seconds and 30-minute register. As a result, the dial is rendered more symmetrical and, along with its round pushers and screw-down case back, bears similarities to Patek Philippe's celebrated Ref. 1463.

New York, 13 June, 2007

Pink-gold and stainless-steel chronograph wristwatch with telemeter, tachymeter and register
Ref. 4062
Chronograph 'Anti-Magnetic'
c.1945

US$ 10,000 – 15,000

SOLD US$ 24,000

Reference 4062 was in production from 1942 until around 1963. The model was cased in a variety of metals, ranging from yellow gold, pink gold and stainless steel, as well as stainless-steel and gold combinations. The reference sometimes features a ribbed band. Square pushers complement the thin and elegant case.

Geneva, 14 May, 2014

Rare yellow-gold chronograph wristwatch with register, tachymeter and telemeter
Ref. 4062
Case 539973
Chronograph 'Anti-Magnetique'
c.1945

CHF 25,000 – 35,000
US$ 28,400 – 57,000

SOLD CHF 87,500

Geneva, 14 May, 2017

Square-form yellow-gold chronograph wristwatch with spiral, tachymeter scale and registers
Ref. 8206 Gabus
Chronograph
c.1945

CHF 40,000 – 60,000
US$ 40,600 – 61,000

SOLD CHF 43,750

Reference 8206 – nicknamed 'Gabus' – is believed to have been produced only in yellow gold and pink gold during the 1940s, and then only in a very limited numbers, making it a highly sought-after piece by avid vintage Rolex collectors today.

Geneva, 13 November, 2018

Pink-gold chronograph wristwatch
Ref. 6032
Chronograph
c.1961

CHF 15,000 – 25,000

SOLD CHF 37,500

Reference 6032 is an extremely rare Rolex chronograph that can be dated to around 1950. The dial has an unusual configuration of Arabic and faceted disc numerals. This reference is one of the few chronographs to be fitted with a Super Oyster crown. As Ref. 6032 has two chronograph registers, it is possible that the model was manufactured for a very short period of time and discontinued in favour of the three-register Ref. 6034.

Geneva, 16 May, 2006

Stainless-steel chronograph
wristwatch with register
Ref. 6034
Oyster
Chronograph
c.1955

CHF 28,000 – 35,000
US$ 21,600 – 27,000

SOLD CHF 66,000

It is interesting to note that the three-register Oyster chronographs made before the introduction of the Daytona were manufactured for only short periods of time. New references were introduced in relatively quick succession, including 5034, 6034, 6234 and 6238. As a consequence, production numbers for these chronographs were comparatively low.

New York, 17 October, 2008

Stainless-steel chronograph
wristwatch with register,
tachymeter, telemeter
and bracelet
Ref. 6034
Chronograph
c.1952

US$ 35,000 – 45,000

NOT SOLD

New York, 17 October, 2008

Stainless-steel chronograph
wristwatch with register,
tachymeter and telemeter
Ref. 6034
Chronograph
c.1952

US$ 35,000 – 45,000

NOT SOLD

Geneva, 16 November, 2004

Stainless-steel chronograph wristwatch with register
Ref. 6234
Oyster
Chronograph 'Anti-Magnetic'
c.1960

CHF 12,000 – 15,000
US$ 9,600 – 11,900

SOLD CHF 33,600

The Ref. 6234 was released in 1955 and produced until 1961. This reference holds a significant place in the Rolex heritage as its natural technical improvements led the brand to design and release the Daytona in 1963. The total production for this reference in stainless steel is estimated to be approximately 2,300 pieces.

New York, 17 October, 2008

Stainless-steel chronograph
wristwatch with registers,
tachymeter and bracelet
Ref. 6234
Chronograph
c.1957

US$ 25,000 – 35,000

SOLD US$ 31,250

Geneva, 16 November, 2008

Stainless-steel chronograph
wristwatch with registers,
tachymeter and bracelet
Ref. 6234
Oyster
Chronograph
c.1965

CHF 25,000 – 35,000
US$ 22,400 – 31,400

SOLD CHF 56,250

Geneva, 16 November, 2004

Stainless-steel chronograph
wristwatch with register
and bracelet
Ref. 6238
'Pre-Daytona' Chronograph
c.1960

CHF 12,000 – 18,000
US$ 9,600 – 14,300

SOLD CHF 20,400

Reference 6238 is referred to by collectors as the 'Pre-Daytona', since it is immediately followed by Ref. 6239, which was the first Cosmograph Daytona ever released. Ref. 6238 is an important model in the history of Rolex as it marks the turning point in the transition from the older classical chronographs to the modern ones. The 'Pre-Daytonas' were only produced for a short period of time during the '60s and are, therefore, quite rare.

New York, 13 June, 2007

Stainless-steel chronograph
wristwatch with registers
and bracelet
Retailed by Tiffany & Co.
Ref. 6238
'Pre-Daytona' Chronograph
*c.*1958

US$ 15,000 – 20,000

SOLD US$ 48,000

New York, 13 June, 2007

Extremely rare stainless-steel
chronograph wristwatch
with black dial, tachymeter,
registers and bracelet
Ref. 6238
'Pre-Daytona' Chronograph
*c.*1960

US$ 30,000 – 50,000

SOLD US$ 129,600

New York, 19 October, 2007

Extremely rare stainless-steel
chronograph wristwatch with
black dial, tachymeter, registers
and bracelet
Ref. 6238
'Pre-Daytona' Chronograph
*c.*1960

US$ 100,000 – 150,000

SOLD US$ 121,000

New York, 23 April, 2008

Stainless-steel chronograph
wristwatch with tachymeter,
registers and bracelet
Ref. 6238
'Pre-Daytona' Chronograph
c.1960

US$ 50,000 – 70,000

SOLD US$ 38,000

This watch belonged to Major League baseball player, Alphonso E. 'Al' Downing. A pitcher for the New York Yankees, he was the American League Strikeout Champion in 1964.

New York, 23 April, 2008

Stainless-steel chronograph
wristwatch with tachymeter
and registers
Ref. 6238
'Pre-Daytona' Chronograph
c.1960

US$ 25,000 – 35,000

SOLD US$ 43,000

New York, 17 October, 2008

Stainless-steel chronograph
wristwatch with black dial, registers,
tachymeter scale and bracelet
Ref. 6238
'Pre-Daytona' Chronograph
c.1959

US$ 100,000 – 150,000

NOT SOLD

Geneva, 13 November, 2012

Very rare stainless-steel chronograph wristwatch with registers and pulsometer scale
Ref. 6238
Case 1106339
'Pre-Daytona' Chronograph
c.1965

CHF 60,000 – 90,000
US$ 64,500 – 96,500

SOLD CHF 68,500

New York, 10 December, 2015

Very rare yellow-gold chronograph wristwatch with registers and tachymeter
Ref. 6238
Case 997150
'Pre-Daytona' Chronograph
c.1963

US$ 40,000 – 60,000
€ 35,000 – 53,000
HK$ 311,000 – 466,000

SOLD US$ 75,000

London, 8 March, 2016

Rare stainless-steel chronograph
wristwatch with registers and bracelet
Ref. 6238
Case 974290
'Pre-Daytona' Chronograph
*c.*1963

£ 10,000 – 15,000
€ 13,200 – 19,700
US$ 14,300 – 21,400

SOLD £ 20,625

Geneva, 13 May, 2018

Rare yellow-gold chronograph
wristwatch with registers and bracelet
Ref. 6238
Case 1422499
'Pre-Daytona' Chronograph
c.1966

CHF 65,000 – 95,000
US$ 68,000 – 99,000

SOLD CHF 81,250

ROLEX
COSMOGRAPH
DAYTONA
T SWISS T

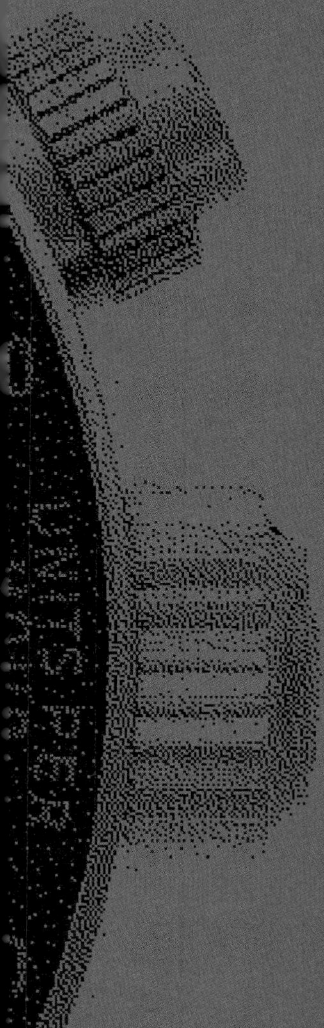

COSMOGRAPH DAYTONA

The first Daytona – Ref. 6239 – was introduced in the early 1960s; it was to set the standards for Rolex chronographs for nearly 25 years. This watch was made to be the most reliable, precise and easy to read.

The movement, based on the Valjoux 72, was gradually upgraded to achieve the ultimate precision. The dial was produced with contrasting subsidiary counters to facilitate easy and accurate reading. For the same reason, the tachymeter scale was moved from the dial to the bezel. The watch also featured proven elements, such as the Oyster bracelet and the screw-down crown and case back. The result was a robust yet elegant sports tool watch.

It is, today, regarded as the most iconic and collectible wristwatch ever produced.

The vintage Daytona world is vast and certain references and characteristics are particularly sought-after. The reference 6239 is perhaps the most renowned.

The watch shown opposite is equipped with its original three-colour 'Paul Newman' dial. Nonetheless, what collectors appreciate is the most-attractive natural 'tropical' patina of the subsidiary dials. Over the years, their colour has changed from black to an appealing shade of 'toffee' brown. This phenomenon is caused by the reaction of materials in the dial to elements such as the sun and other forms of light. Note that the white part of the dial has also turned to an attractive cream colour.

The original owner wearing the watch.

Very few examples of a Rolex 'Paul Newman' with such an appealing patina are known. What was originally considered to be a defect has become, today, highly desirable and coveted.

This watch was consigned to auction by its original and only owner. This piece came with an incredibly full set, comprising the original guarantee, invoice, box and outer packaging.

The watch was originally purchased new as a gift in 1975, by which time it was already seven years old and had a price tag of only £134.

The name 'Cosmograph' was first used on another Rolex watch: the Ref. 6062 Oyster Perpetual with moon phases and triple date, which was produced from 1950 to 1953. At the time it was called 'Cosmograph' because the moon phases were indicated against the backdrop of a dark blue starry sky. The name was then used again in 1963 to designate this new chronograph, a reference to the various space conquests that so fascinated the world in the late 1950s.

Geneva, 13 May, 2018

Very rare stainless-steel chronograph wristwatch with registers, 'tropical' subsidiary dials and bracelet
Ref. 6239
Case 2004742
Cosmograph Daytona
*c.*1969

CHF 200,000 – 400,000
US$ 208,000 – 416,000

SOLD CHF 951,000

Geneva, 16 November, 2004

Stainless-steel chronograph wristwatch with registers and bracelet
Ref. 6239
Cosmograph Daytona
'Paul Newman'
*c.*1965

CHF 22,000 – 28,000
US$ 17,500 – 22,200

SOLD CHF 45,600

Geneva, 15 November, 2005

Gold chronograph
wristwatch with registers
Ref. 6239
Cosmograph Daytona
'Paul Newman'
c.1965

CHF 35,000 – 45,000
US$ 22,400 – 28,800

SOLD CHF 66,000

Geneva, 15 November, 2005

Rare stainless-steel chronograph
wristwatch with registers
Made for the Peruvian air force
Ref. 6239
Oyster
Cosmograph Daytona
c.1960

CHF 20,000 – 30,000
US$ 12,900 – 19,300

SOLD CHF 26,400

New York, 5 December, 2005

Stainless-steel chronograph
wristwatch with registers
Ref. 6239
Cosmograph Daytona
c.1967

US$ 30,000 – 35,000

SOLD US$ 45,000

Geneva, 16 May, 2006

Stainless-steel chronograph
wristwatch with registers
and bracelet
Ref. 6239
Cosmograph Daytona
'Paul Newman'
c.1967

CHF 30,000 – 40,000
US$ 23,100 – 30,800

SOLD CHF 36,000

1 New York, 8 June, 2006

Stainless-steel chronograph wristwatch with registers, tachymeter and bracelet
Ref. 6239
Cosmograph Daytona
'Paul Newman'
*c.*1966

US$ 40,000 – 50,000

SOLD US$ 69,000

2 New York, 23 April, 2008

Stainless-steel chronograph wristwatch with registers, tachymeter and bracelet
Ref. 6239/6262
Cosmograph Daytona
'Paul Newman'
*c.*1967

US$ 50,000 – 70,000

SOLD US$ 79,000

3 New York, 17 October, 2008

Stainless-steel chronograph wristwatch with registers, tachymeter and bracelet
Ref. 6239
Cosmograph Daytona
'Paul Newman'
*c.*1967

US$ 60,000 – 90,000

SOLD US$ 74,500

4 Geneva, 16 November, 2008

Stainless-steel chronograph wristwatch with registers and bracelet
Ref. 6239
Cosmograph Daytona
'Paul Newman'
*c.*1967

CHF 65,000 – 95,000
US$ 58,500 – 85,500

SOLD CHF 74,500

1

2

3

4

1 Geneva, 16 November, 2008

Stainless-steel chronograph wristwatch with registers and bracelet
Ref. 6239
Cosmograph Daytona
'Paul Newman'
*c.*1970

CHF 55,000 – 75,000
US$ 49,300 – 67,500

SOLD CHF 62,500

2 Geneva, 16 November, 2008

Stainless-steel chronograph wristwatch with registers and bracelet
Ref. 6239
Cosmograph Daytona
*c.*1970

CHF 25,000 – 35,000
US$ 22,400 – 31,400

SOLD CHF 28,750

1

2

3 London, 18 December, 2008

Stainless-steel chronograph wristwatch with registers and bracelet
Ref. 6239
Cosmograph Daytona
'Paul Newman'
*c.*1966

£ 30,000 – 40,000
€ 37,600 – 50,500
US$ 46,700 – 62,500

NOT SOLD

3

Geneva, 10 May, 2009

Stainless-steel chronograph
wristwatch with registers
Ref. 6239
Cosmograph Daytona
'Paul Newman'
*c.*1968

CHF 50,000 – 70,000
US$ 44,700 – 63,000

SOLD CHF 62,500

1 Geneva, 14 November, 2010

Rare stainless-steel chronograph wristwatch with registers
Ref. 6239
Cosmograph Daytona
'Paul Newman'
c.1967

CHF 60,000 – 80,000
US$ 61,500 – 81,500

SOLD CHF 68,500

2 Geneva, 15 May, 2011

Rare stainless-steel chronograph wristwatch with registers and bracelet
Ref. 6239/6241
Cosmograph Daytona
'Paul Newman'
c.1966

CHF 50,000 – 70,000
US$ 55,500 – 77,500

SOLD CHF 104,500

3 Geneva, 15 May, 2011

Rare stainless-steel chronograph wristwatch with registers and bracelet
Ref. 6239/6241
Cosmograph Daytona
'Paul Newman'
c.1966

CHF 50,000 – 80,000
US$ 66,500 – 88,500

SOLD CHF 104,500

4 Geneva, 13 November, 2011

Rare stainless-steel chronograph with registers and bracelet
Ref. 6239
Cosmograph Daytona
'Paul Newman'
c.1966

CHF 35,000 – 55,000
US$ 66,500 – 89,000

SOLD CHF 82,900

1

2

3

4

Geneva, 13 November, 2011

Rare yellow-gold chronograph
wristwatch with registers
Ref. 6239
Cosmograph Daytona
'Paul Newman'
c.1966

CHF 50,000 – 60,000
US$ 55,500 – 66,500

SOLD CHF 98,500

Geneva, 15 May, 2012

Rare stainless-steel chronograph
wristwatch with registers and bracelet
Ref. 6239
Cosmograph Daytona
'Paul Newman'
c.1965

CHF 60,000 – 80,000
US$ 66,000 – 88,000

SOLD CHF 74,500

Geneva, 12 November, 2013

Rare stainless-steel chronograph
wristwatch with registers and
tachymeter
Ref. 6239
Case 1997793
Cosmograph Daytona
'Paul Newman'
c.1969

CHF 60,000 – 80,000
US$ 65,000 – 86,500

SOLD CHF 118,750

New York, 10 December, 2013

Stainless-steel chronograph with registers
Ref. 6239
Case 1626980
Cosmograph Daytona
'Paul Newman'
c.1962

US$ 35,000 – 55,000
€ 25,900 – 40,700
HK$ 272,000 – 427,000

SOLD US$ 112,500

Geneva, 14 May, 2014

Stainless-steel chronograph wristwatch with registers, tachymeter and bracelet
Ref. 6239
Case 1192375
Cosmograph Daytona
'Paul Newman'
c.1965

CHF 60,000 – 80,000
US$ 68,500 – 91,000

SOLD CHF 203,000

Geneva, 14 May, 2014

Rare stainless-steel chronograph wristwatch with registers and tachymeter
Ref. 6239/6242
Case 2048275
Cosmograph Daytona
'Paul Newman'
c.1969

CHF 60,000 – 80,000
US$ 68,500 – 91,000

SOLD CHF 93,750

Geneva, 14 May, 2014

Rare stainless-steel chronograph wristwatch with registers and tachymeter
Ref. 6239
Case 1626936
Cosmograph Daytona
'Paul Newman'
c.1966

CHF 60,000 – 80,000
US$ 68,500 – 91,000

SOLD CHF 90,000

Geneva, 13 May, 2015

Stainless-steel chronograph
wristwatch with bracelet
Ref. 6239
Case 2004674
Cosmograph Daytona
'Paul Newman'
c.1968

CHF 60,000 – 80,000
US$ 61,500 – 82,000

SOLD CHF 115,000

Geneva, 13 May, 2015

Rare stainless-steel chronograph
wristwatch with registers,
tachymeter and bracelet
Ref. 6239
Case 1626266
Cosmograph Daytona
'Paul Newman'
c.1963

CHF 50,000 – 60,000
US$ 51,500 – 61,500

SOLD CHF 87,500

New York, 24 May, 2018

Stainless-steel chronograph
wristwatch with registers and bracelet
Ref. 6239
Case 1958606
Cosmograph Daytona
'Paul Newman'
c.1969

US$ 70,000 – 100,000
€ 57,000 – 81,500
HK$ 550,000 – 785,000

SOLD US$ 112,500

New York, 5 December, 2018

Stainless-steel chronograph
wristwatch
Ref. 6239
Cosmograph Daytona
'Paul Newman'
c.1970

US$ 125,000 – 225,000
€ 110,000 – 197,000
HK$ 980,000 – 1,770,000

SOLD US$ 175,000

Geneva, 12 May, 2019

Stainless-steel chronograph wristwatch
with bracelet
Ref. 6239
Cosmograph Daytona
'Paul Newman'
c.1968

CHF 80,000 – 120,000
US$ 80,000 – 120,000

SOLD CHF 125,000

New York, 4 June, 2019

Stainless-steel chronograph
wristwatch with registers and
bracelet
Ref. 6239
Cosmograph Daytona
c.1969

US$ 100,000 – 150,000
€ 88,500 – 133,000
HK$ 785,000 – 1,180,000

SOLD US$ 181,250

Geneva, 13 November, 2018

Stainless-steel chronograph
wristwatch with pulsometer
Ref. 6239
Cosmograph Daytona
c.1967

CHF 500,000 – 1,000,000
US$ 505,000 – 1,010,000

SOLD CHF 831,000

Made in 1967, this watch is the third known example of a Rolex red Daytona Ref. 6239 fitted with such an extraordinary pulsations dial. The medical Daytona is one of the rarest chronographs ever made. There are very subtle variations between each of the dials that also make this example so exciting. The black scale has been completely redesigned to make room for the external blue pulsations scale graduated for 15 beats and the applied numerals have been moved closer to the centre of the dial to make space for the additional calibrations. This super rare watch with bright blue pulsations scale found along the outer edge of the dial is amazing. The lumes are intact and have aged to a pleasant golden brown. The case is very crisp with good proportions and incredibly sharp and easy-to-read numbers between the lugs.

1 Geneva, 13 May, 2015

Rare stainless-steel chronograph wristwatch with colour-changed registers, tachymeter and bracelet
Ref. 6240
Case 1659519
Cosmograph Daytona
c.1967

CHF 30,000 – 50,000
US$ 30,700 – 51,500

SOLD CHF 56,250

2 Geneva, 13 November, 2018

Stainless-steel chronograph wristwatch with tropical registers and bracelet
Ref. 6240
Cosmograph Daytona 'Jumbo'
c.1966

CHF 150,000 – 300,000
US$ 152,000 – 303,000

SOLD CHF 187,500

Ref. 6240 was first introduced in the mid 1960s. Not considered a commercial success (there were numerus complaints about the size of the crowns and pushers), it was discontinued in 1969. Early batches of this reference feature a rare dial known as the 'Jumbo' Daytona. Rolex experimented with different dial configurations before becoming satisfied with the references 6263 and 6265. While earlier Daytona models featured a small 'Daytona' script below 'Rolex Cosmograph', Rolex also introduced a different dial configuration displaying a slightly larger 'Daytona' font.

1

2

1 Geneva, 12 May, 2019

Stainless-steel chronograph wristwatch with bracelet and tropical registers
Property from an important international collector
Ref. 6240
Cosmograph Daytona
'Jumbo'
c.1966

CHF 100,000 – 200,000
US$ 100,000 – 200,000

NOT SOLD

2 Geneva, 12 November, 2019

Stainless-steel chronograph wristwatch with bracelet
Ref. 6240
Case 1'658'509
Cosmograph Daytona
'Paul Newman'
c.1967

CHF 160,000 – 300,000
US$ 161,000 – 302,000

NOT SOLD

1

2

New York, 17 October, 2008

Stainless-steel chronograph wristwatch with registers, tachymeter and bracelet
Ref. 6241
Cosmograph Daytona
'Paul Newman'
c.1967

US$ 80,000 – 120,000

NOT SOLD

Ref. 6241 was only in production from 1965 to 1969. During that time, Rolex produced approximately 2,700 pieces, of which a very limited number were fitted with an exotic dial. This feature later became known as the 'Paul Newman' dial, and is characterised by the square markers in the chronograph scale and subsidiary dials, as well as the alternating patterning of the colouration. To the best of our knowledge, the majority of reference 6241s were made with stainless-steel cases, though 400 pieces were made in 14k yellow gold, and 300 pieces were made in 18k yellow gold.

New York, 17 October, 2008

Rare yellow-gold chronograph wristwatch with registers and tachymeter
Ref. 6241
Cosmograph Daytona
'Paul Newman'
*c.*1967

US$ 100,000 – 150,000

NOT SOLD

Geneva, 15 May, 2011

Rare stainless-steel chronograph wristwatch with registers and bracelet
Ref. 6241
Cosmograph Daytona
'Paul Newman'
*c.*1965

CHF 65,000 – 85,000
US$ 72,000 – 94,000

SOLD CHF 122,500

Geneva, 13 November, 2012

Rare stainless-steel chronograph wristwatch with registers and bracelet
Ref. 6241
Case 2372750
Cosmograph Daytona
'Paul Newman'
c.1970

CHF 40,000 – 60,000
US$ 42,700 – 64,500

SOLD CHF 56,250

Geneva, 11 May, 2013

Rare stainless-steel chronograph wristwatch with registers and bracelet
Ref. 6241
Case 2036628
Cosmograph Daytona
'Paul Newman'
c.1969

CHF 50,000 – 80,000
US$ 53,000 – 85,000

SOLD CHF 75,000

New York, 10 June, 2013

Rare yellow-gold chronograph
wristwatch with registers
and bracelet
Ref. 6241
Case 2084264
Cosmograph Daytona
'Paul Newman'
*c.*1964

US$ 50,000 – 70,000
€ 38,400 – 54,000
HK$ 389,000 – 545,000

SOLD US$ 185,000

Geneva, 12 November, 2013

Rare yellow-gold chronograph
wristwatch with registers
and tachymeter
Ref. 6241
Case 1947414
Cosmograph Daytona
'Paul Newman'
*c.*1966

CHF 60,000 – 80,000
US$ 65,000 – 86,500

SOLD CHF 197,000

New York, 10 December, 2014

Rare stainless-steel chronograph
wristwatch with registers and bracelet
Ref. 6241
Case 1764971
Cosmograph Daytona
'Paul Newman'
*c.*1964

US$ 60,000 – 80,000
€ 47,800 – 64,000
HK$ 466,000 – 625,000

SOLD US$ 131,000

New York, 10 December, 2015

Very rare yellow-gold chronograph
wristwatch with registers and
tachymeter
Ref. 6241
Case 2084228
Cosmograph Daytona
'Paul Newman'
*c.*1968

US$ 80,000 – 120,000
€ 71,000 – 106,000
HK$ 625,000 – 935,000

SOLD US$ 250,000

1 London, 8 March, 2016

Very rare yellow-gold chronograph wristwatch with registers and tachymeter
Ref. 6241
Case 2084311
Cosmograph Daytona
'Paul Newman'
c.1969

£ 60,000 – 80,000
€ 79,000 – 105,000
US$ 86,000 – 115,000

SOLD £ 137,000

1

2

2 London, 8 March, 2016

Rare stainless-steel chronograph wristwatch with registers and bracelet
Ref. 6241
Case 1767488
Cosmograph Daytona
'Paul Newman'
c.1970

£ 40,000 – 60,000
€ 52,500 – 79,000
US$ 57,500 – 86,000

SOLD £ 102,500

3 Geneva, 13 November, 2018

Stainless-steel chronograph wristwatch with bracelet and brown registers
Case 6241
Cosmograph Daytona
'Paul Newman'
c.1968

CHF 120,000 – 180,000
US$ 122,000 – 182,000

SOLD CHF 287,500

3

Geneva, 16 November, 2004

Stainless-steel chronograph
wristwatch with registers
and bracelet
Ref. 6262
Cosmograph Daytona
'Paul Newman'
c.1968

CHF 22,000 – 28,000
US$ 17,500 – 22,200

SOLD CHF 42,000

Known as a transitional reference, the Rolex Daytona 6262 had a notably short production run, lasting only from the late 1960s to c.1972. Although extremely similar in appearance to Ref. 6239, the 6262 is fitted with an improved Valjoux movement, Calibre 727. Having evolved from Calibre 722-1, Rolex improved the 727's performance by changing the balance from 18'000 to 21'600 vibrations per hour, which noticeably increased the precision.

Geneva, 17 May, 2005

Stainless-steel chronograph wristwatch with registers and bracelet
Ref. 6262
Cosmograph Daytona
'Paul Newman'
*c.*1968

CHF 25,000 – 35,000
US$ 16,200 – 22,600

SOLD CHF 40,800

Geneva, 15 November, 2005

Stainless-steel chronograph wristwatch with registers
Ref. 6262
Cosmograph Daytona
'Paul Newman'
*c.*1968

CHF 28,000 – 35,000
US$ 18,000 – 22,500

SOLD CHF 50,400

Geneva, 16 May, 2006

Stainless-steel chronograph wristwatch with registers and bracelet
Ref. 6262
Cosmograph Daytona
'Paul Newman'
*c.*1968

CHF 30,000 – 40,000
US$ 23,100 – 30,800

SOLD CHF 36,000

1 Geneva, 14 November, 2010

Rare stainless-steel chronograph wrist-watch with registers and bracelet
Ref. 6262/6239
Cosmograph Daytona
'Paul Newman'
*c.*1970

CHF 60,000 – 80,000
US$ 61,500 – 81,500

SOLD CHF 104,500

2 Geneva, 15 May, 2011

Rare stainless-steel chronograph wristwatch with registers
Ref. 6262/6241
Oyster
Cosmograph Daytona
'Paul Newman'
*c.*1967

CHF 65,000 – 85,000
US$ 72,000 – 94,000

SOLD CHF 116,500

1

2

3 Geneva, 13 November, 2011

Rare stainless-steel chronograph wristwatch with registers and bracelet
Ref. 6262
Cosmograph Daytona
'Paul Newman'
*c.*1968

CHF 60,000 – 80,000
US$ 66,500 – 89,000

SOLD CHF 74,500

4 Geneva, 13 November, 2012

Rare stainless-steel chronograph wristwatch with registers
Ref. 6262/6239
Case 2547520
Cosmograph Daytona
'Chocolate dial'
*c.*1970

CHF 35,000 – 55,000
US$ 37,400 – 59,000

SOLD CHF 56,250

3

4

1 Geneva, 13 November, 2012

Rare stainless-steel chronograph
wristwatch with colour-changed
registers and bracelet
Ref. 6262/6263 Case 2733498
Cosmograph Daytona
c.1971

CHF 37,000 – 47,000
US$ 39,500 – 56,250

SOLD CHF 27,500

2 New York, 10 December, 2014

Stainless-steel chronograph
wristwatch with bracelet
Ref. 6262 Case 2475267
Cosmograph Daytona
'Paul Newman'
c.1968

US$ 50,000 – 60,000

SOLD US$ 106,250

1

2

3 Geneva, 10 November, 2015

Rare stainless-steel chronograph
wristwatch with registers
and bracelet
Ref. 6262 Case 2415797
Cosmograph Daytona
'Paul Newman'
c.1971

CHF 60,000 – 80,000
US$ 61,500 – 82,000

SOLD CHF 100,000

4 London, 8 March, 2016

Rare stainless-steel chronograph
wristwatch with colour-changed
registers and bracelet
Ref. 6262/6239 Case 2475491
Cosmograph Daytona
c.1970

£ 25,000 – 35,000
€ 32,800 – 46,000
US$ 35,700 – 50,000

SOLD £ 38,750

3

4

London, 8 March, 2016

Rare stainless-steel chronograph wristwatch with registers and bracelet
Ref. 6262
Case 2321021
Cosmograph Daytona
'Paul Newman'
c.1970

£ 25,000 – 55,000
€ 46,000 – 72,500
US$ 50,000 – 78,500

SOLD £ 68,750

London, 19 September, 2017

Rare stainless-steel chronograph wristwatch with registers and bracelet
Ref. 6262
Case 2527538
Cosmograph Daytona
'Paul Newman'
c.1970

£ 50,000 – 80,000
€ 56,500 – 90,000
US$ 65,500 – 105,000

SOLD £ 143,750

Geneva, 12 May, 2019

Stainless-steel chronograph wristwatch
with bracelet
Ref. 6262
Cosmograph Daytona
'Paul Newman'
c.1970

CHF 80,000 – 120,000
US$ 80,000 – 120,000

SOLD CHF 212,500

Geneva, 16 November, 2004

Stainless-steel chronograph
wristwatch with registers
Ref. 6263
Cosmograph Daytona
'Paul Newman'
c.1975

CHF 22,000 – 28,000
US$ 17,500 – 22,200

SOLD CHF 54,000

The reference 6263 was one of the last manually-wound stainless-steel Daytona chronographs in production until Rolex replaced it with automatic versions in 1988.

The 6263 was given its own distinctive look with the addition of a black acrylic insert to its bezel and a new set of pushers, which were now screw-down and, therefore, waterproof. Ref. 6263 was manufactured for almost twenty years.

Geneva, 17 May, 2005

Stainless-steel chronograph
wristwatch with register
Ref. 6263
Oyster
Cosmograph Daytona
'Paul Newman'
*c.*1972

CHF 28,000 – 35,000
US$ 18,100 – 22,600

SOLD CHF 51,600

Geneva, 17 May, 2005

Steel chronograph wristwatch
with registers and bracelet
Ref. 6263
Oyster
Cosmograph Daytona
*c.*1980

CHF 35,000 – 45,000
US$ 22,600 – 29,000

SOLD CHF 42,000

Geneva, 17 May, 2005

Stainless-steel chronograph
wristwatch with registers
and bracelet
Ref. 6263
Oyster
Cosmograph Daytona
'Paul Newman'
c.1982

CHF 14,000 – 18,000
€ 9,100 – 11,600

SOLD CHF 26,400

Geneva, 17 May, 2005

Gold chronograph wristwatch
with registers and bracelet
Ref. 6263
Oyster
Cosmograph Daytona
c.1979

CHF 30,000 – 40,000
US$ 19,400 – 25,800

SOLD CHF 40,800

Geneva, 15 November, 2005

Stainless-steel chronograph wristwatch with register and bracelet
Ref. 6263
Oyster
Cosmograph Daytona
c.1971

CHF 14,000 – 18,000
US$ 9,000 – 11,600

SOLD CHF 24,000

Geneva, 15 May, 2007

Gold chronograph wristwatch with registers
Ref. 6263
Cosmograph Daytona
c.1985

CHF 30,000 – 40,000
US$ 24,900 – 33,100

SOLD CHF 72,000

New York, 23 April, 2008

Rare stainless-steel chronograph wristwatch with registers, tachymeter and bracelet
Ref. 6263/6262
Oyster
Cosmograph Daytona 'Albino'
c.1971

US$ 100,000 – 150,000

SOLD US$ 505,000

This watch has an interesting provenance, having been purchased at auction in 2003 at the Christie's sale of the Eric Clapton Collection before being sold on again in 2008.

During the period that this watch was produced – late 1960s to late '80s – the standard dial design for a Cosmograph Daytona featured either a black background with lighter-coloured subsidiary dials or the inverse with lighter background and black subsidiaries.

This example is from a little-known and exceptionally rare variation, known as the 'Albino', in which both the background and subsidiary dials are all in a monochrome silver colour. This design harks back to the dials of the pre-Daytonas, Ref. 6238, which featured only one colour. The 'Albino' combines the tonal simplicity of those dials with the more minimal style of the Daytona face, with the tachymeter scale pushed out to the bezel.

Such examples are significantly rarer than 'Paul Newman' models and very rarely appear at auction or anywhere on the watch market.

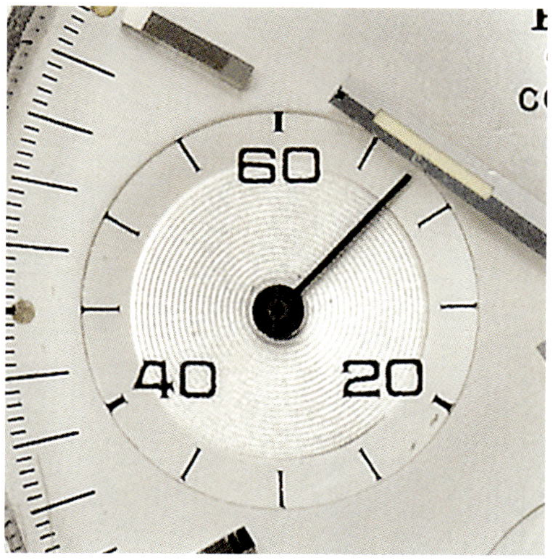

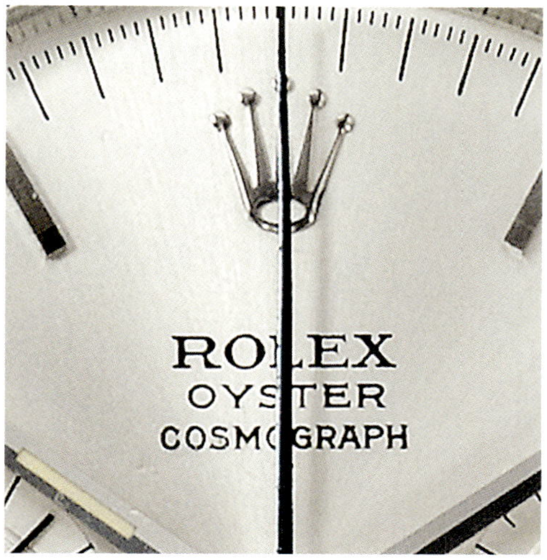

London, 16 July, 2008

Stainless-steel chronograph
wristwatch with registers
and bracelet
Ref. 6263
Oyster
Cosmograph Daytona
c.1983

£ 14,000 – 18,000
€ 17,600 – 22,600
US$ 27,700 – 35,600

SOLD £ 25,000

Geneva, 16 November, 2008

Stainless-steel chronograph
wristwatch with registers
and bracelet
Ref. 6263
Oyster
Cosmograph Daytona
c.1967

CHF 22,000 – 28,000
US$ 19,700 – 25,100

SOLD CHF 28,750

Geneva, 16 November, 2008

Yellow-gold chronograph wristwatch with registers and bracelet
Ref. 6263
Oyster
Cosmograph Daytona
c.1980

CHF 25,000 – 35,000
US$ 22,400 – 31,400

SOLD CHF 63,700

Geneva, 15 November, 2009

Rare 18k yellow-gold chronograph wristwatch with registers and bracelet
Ref. 6263
Oyster
Cosmograph Daytona
c.1974

CHF 40,000 – 60,000
US$ 38,800 – 58,500

SOLD CHF 80,500

Geneva, 15 November, 2009

Rare 18k yellow-gold chronograph wristwatch with register and bracelet
Ref. 6263
Oyster
Cosmograph Daytona
'Paul Newman'
*c.*1984

CHF 70,000 – 90,000
US$ 68,000 – 87,500

SOLD CHF 86,500

Geneva, 14 November, 2010

Rare stainless-steel chronograph wristwatch with registers and date
Ref. 6263/6239
Oyster
Cosmograph Daytona
'Paul Newman'
*c.*1966

CHF 60,000 – 80,000
US$ 61,500 – 81,500

SOLD CHF 254,500

Geneva, 14 November, 2010

Very rare stainless-steel chronograph wristwatch with brown dial, registers and bracelet
Ref. 6263/6239
Oyster
Cosmograph Daytona
'Paul Newman'
c.1969

CHF 60,000 – 80,000
US$ 61,500 – 81,500

SOLD CHF 464,500

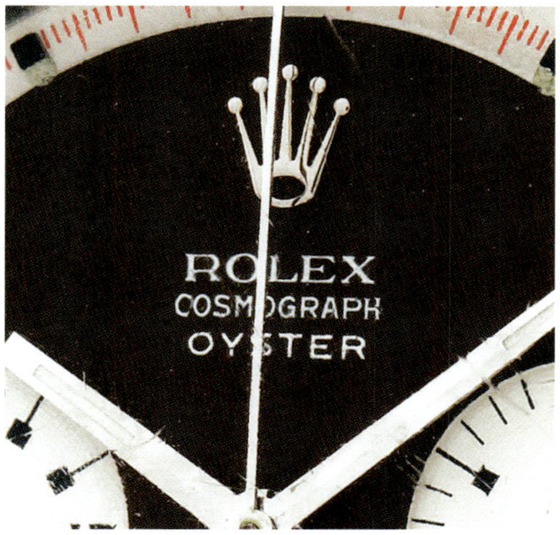

Geneva, 15 May, 2011

Stainless-steel chronograph
wristwatch with registers
and bracelet
Ref. 6263/6262
Oyster
Cosmograph Daytona
c.1969

CHF 35,000 – 45,000
US$ 38,700 – 49,700

SOLD CHF 43,750

Geneva, 15 May, 2011

Extremely rare stainless-steel
chronograph wristwatch with
registers and bracelet
Ref. 6263/6239
Oyster
Cosmograph Daytona
'Paul Newman'
Inverted lines
c.1967

CHF 100,000 – 150,000
US$ 110,000 – 166,000

SOLD CHF 206,500

Geneva, 13 November, 2011

Rare stainless-steel chronograph
wristwatch with registers and bracelet
Ref. 6263
Cosmograph Daytona
'Paul Newman'
c.1967

CHF 60,000 – 80,000
US$ 66,500 – 89,000

SOLD CHF 104,500

Geneva, 15 May, 2012

Stainless-steel chronograph
wristwatch with colour-changed
registers and bracelet
Ref. 6263/6265
Cosmograph Daytona
c.1970

CHF 40,000 – 60,000
US$ 44,000 – 66,000

SOLD CHF 50,000

Geneva, 13 November, 2012

Rare stainless-steel chronograph wristwatch with registers
Ref. 6263/6262
Case 2874354
Cosmograph Daytona
'Paul Newman'
c.1970

CHF 60,000 – 80,000
US$ 64,500 – 85,500

SOLD CHF 140,500

Geneva, 11 May, 2013

18k-gold chronograph wristwatch with registers
Ref. 6263
Case 5035107
Cosmograph Daytona
c.1977

CHF 30,000 – 40,000
US$ 31,800 – 42,400

SOLD CHF 50,000

Geneva, 14 May, 2014

Rare stainless-steel chronograph
wristwatch with registers,
tachymeter and bracelet
Ref. 6263/6262
Case 3048318
Cosmograph Daytona
'Paul Newman'
'Panda' dial
c.1972

CHF 250,000 – 500,000
US$ 284,000 – 570,000

SOLD CHF 359,000

New York, 10 December, 2014

Rare stainless-steel chronograph wristwatch with bracelet
Ref. 6263
Case 2874356
Cosmograph Daytona
'Paul Newman'
'Panda' dial
c.1975

US$ 150,000 – 200,000
€ 120,000 – 160,000

SOLD US$ 185,000

The most sought-after configuration of the Paul Newman dials is nicknamed 'Panda'. It is characterised by a white dial contrasting with black subsidiary dials and black outer minute ring.

New York, 24 May, 2018

Rare stainless-steel chronograph wristwatch with registers and bracelet
Ref. 6263
Case 2653820
Oyster
Cosmograph Daytona
c.1971

US$ 80,000 – 120,000
€ 65,000 – 97,500

SOLD US$ 87,500

Geneva, 13 November, 2018

Stainless-steel chronograph wristwatch with dial and bracelet
Ref. 6263
Cosmograph Daytona
'Paul Newman'
c.1970

CHF 300,000 – 600,000
US$ 303,000 – 610,000

NOT SOLD

The 'NOS' Rolex Daytona Reference 6263

A pair of new old stock watches.

These two watches are in such extraordinary and unused condition that they can literally be used by collectors to study and discover how the Rolex Daytona Ref. 6263 would have left the retail shop.

The cases, dials and bracelets have never been used or worn and the case backs both bear a brand new green Rolex factory sticker. In addition, the watches are accompanied by their original guarantees, stamped by the same Swiss retailer on the very same day.

Virtually impossible to find in this state, this extraordinary pair were last seen on the market at the groundbreaking Rolex Daytona-themed 'Lesson One' sale in 2013 and since then they have been sleeping with the same International collector. This pair is still as close to factory finish as any collector will ever be able to find. [See opposite and overleaf]

ROLEX
OYSTER
COSMOGRAPH
DAYTONA
UNITS PER HOUR
ROLEX
OYSTER
COSMOGRAPH
DAYTONA
UNITS PER HOUR

Geneva, 13 November, 2018

Stainless-steel chronograph
wristwatch with bracelet
Ref. 6263
Cosmograph Daytona
'Big Red
c.1984

CHF 120,000 – 250,000
US$ 122,000 – 253,000

SOLD CHF 187,500

Geneva, 13 November, 2018

Stainless-steel chronograph
wristwatch with bracelet
Ref. 6263
Cosmograph Daytona
'Big Red'
c.1983

CHF 120,000 – 250,000
US$ 122,000 – 253,000

SOLD CHF 187,500

Geneva, 13 November, 2018

Stainless-steel chronograph wristwatch with bracelet
Ref. 6263
Oyster 'Sotto'
Cosmograph Daytona
'Paul Newman'
c.1969

CHF 500,000 – 1,000,000
US$ 505,000 – 1,010,000

NOT SOLD

This extremely rare Rolex reference 6263 'Oyster Sotto Paul Newman' is arguably one of the most sought-after models from the famed Swiss brand. A variant of the already incredibly popular 'Paul Newman' Daytona, it carries a black dial and the correct corresponding signature on it. 'Sotto' translates from Italian to 'underneath' and refers to the placement of the word 'Oyster' on the dial for a Ref. 6263 'Paul Newman' with black dial.

Most Ref. 6263 Daytonas were furnished with a white dial; only an estimated total of fewer than 20 pieces appeared with the black Oyster 'Sotto' dial. This attractive example has very faint signs of ageing to the dial, in particular to the subsidiary registers, which have an outer black ring like many of the other known 'Oyster Sottos'. The case number is also in line with other examples, beginning with 2,085 million.

This example is fitted with the correct pushers, the correct insert and further stamped '6239' inside the case back.

New York, 5 December, 2018

Rare yellow-gold chronograph
wristwatch with bracelet
Retailed by Tiffany & Co.
Ref. 6263
Cosmograph Daytona
c.1974

US$ 120,000 – 220,000
€ 106,000 – 193,000
HK$ 945,000 – 1,730,000

SOLD US$ 150,000

Geneva, 12 November, 2019

Stainless-steel chronograph
wristwatch with bracelet
Ref. 6263
Case 2'085'601
Cosmograph Daytona
'Paul Newman'
'Panda' dial
c.1969

CHF 300,000 – 500,000
US$ 302,000 – 505,000

SOLD CHF 412,500

1 Geneva, 16 November, 2004

Stainless-steel chronograph
wristwatch with registers
and bracelet
Ref. 6264
Cosmograph Daytona
'Paul Newman'
*c.*1965

CHF 22,000 – 28,000
US$ 17,500 – 22,200

SOLD CHF 63,600

2 Geneva, 13 November, 2011

Rare stainless-steel chronograph wrist-
watch with registers and bracelet
Ref. 6264/6241
Cosmograph Daytona
'Paul Newman'
*c.*1967

CHF 100,000 – 150,000
US$ 111,000 – 167,000

SOLD CHF 122,500

Launched in 1970 alongside Ref. 6262, the 6264 is among the rarest of all Daytona references due to its short production span of only one year. The two models can be distinguished by the different types of bezels. While the 6262 is fitted with an engraved solid steel bezel, the 6264 comes with a black acrylic bezel insert. Equipped with pump pushers, the 6264 looks identical to its predecessor reference 6241 and only differs by the movement used. Instead of the calibre 722 with 18,000 beats per hour, the faster and newer calibre 727 was used, vibrating 21,600 times per hour.

1

2

Geneva, 13 November, 2011

Rare yellow-gold chronograph wristwatch with registers
Ref. 6264/6241
Cosmograph Daytona
'Paul Newman'
c.1967

CHF 100,000 – 150,000
US$ 111,000 – 167,000

NOT SOLD

Geneva, 15 May, 2012

Rare stainless-steel chronograph wristwatch with registers and bracelet
Ref. 6264/6241
Cosmograph Daytona
'Paul Newman'
c.1967

CHF 60,000 – 80,000
US$ 66,000 – 88,000

SOLD CHF 74,500

Hong Kong, 2 April, 2018

Very fine and extremely rare yellow-gold chronograph wristwatch with registers and tropical minute track
Ref. 6264
Case 2357421
Cosmograph Daytona
'Paul Newman'
'Lemon' dial
c.1970

HK$ 3,200,000 – 6,000,000
US$ 409,000 – 770,000

SOLD HK$ 5,760,000

This watch features a dial nicknamed 'Lemon' by the Rolex community. The configuration of a 'Lemon' dial is uncommon for various reasons: typically the dial should be more of a cream colour, the 'Lemon' dial features a more attractive citrus tone with intense black subsidiary dials and white graphics instead of gilt subsidiary-markers. To the best of our knowledge, there are only a handful of 'Lemon' dials known. What further distinguishes the present example is the outer minute track, which has turned to a very warm 'tropical' brown.

Geneva, 13 November, 2018

Stainless-steel chronograph
wristwatch with bracelet
Ref. 6264
Cosmograph Daytona
'Paul Newman'
'Panda' dial
c.1970

CHF 200,000 – 300,000
US$ 202,000 – 303,000

SOLD CHF 275,000

Geneva, 12 May, 2019

Stainless-steel chronograph
wristwatch with bracelet
Ref. 6264
Cosmograph Daytona
'Paul Newman'
*c.*1970

CHF 140,000 – 240,000
US$ 138,000 – 236,500

SOLD CHF 162,500

Geneva, 16 November, 2004

Gold chronograph wristwatch
with registers
Ref. 6265
Oyster
Cosmograph Daytona
c.1975

CHF 18,000 – 22,000
US$ 14,300 – 17,500

SOLD CHF 36,000

Behind the celebrated name, some references are particularly cherished by collectors. Regarded as the ultimate evolution of the vintage models, the 6265 is undoubtedly one of these. Produced from the early 1970s to 1987, it gathers together some of the most attractive Rolex features, such as a movement based on the Valjoux 72, screw-down chronograph pushers and elegant proportions.

New York, 17 October, 2008

Stainless-steel chronograph
wristwatch with registers,
tachymeter and bracelet
Ref. 6265/6263
Cosmograph Daytona
*c.*1982

US$ 50,000 – 70,000

NOT SOLD

New York, 17 October, 2008

Stainless-steel chronograph wristwatch with registers, tachymeter and bracelet
Ref. 6265
Oyster
Cosmograph Daytona
c.1982

US$ 35,000 – 45,000

NOT SOLD

Geneva, 16 November, 2008

Stainless-steel chronograph wristwatch with registers and bracelet
Ref. 6265
Oyster
Cosmograph Daytona
c.1976

CHF 20,000 – 30,000
US$ 18,000 – 26,900

SOLD CHF 33,750

Geneva, 15 May, 2012

Unusual stainless-steel chronograph wristwatch with gilt registers and bracelet
Ref. 6265
Cosmograph Daytona
*c.*1976

CHF 30,000 – 50,000
US$ 33,000 – 55,000

SOLD CHF 37,500

Geneva, 11 May, 2013

18k yellow-gold chronograph wristwatch with registers and bracelet
Ref. 6265
Case 6123290
Cosmograph Daytona
*c.*1979

CHF 35,000 – 55,000
US$ 37,100 – 58,500

NOT SOLD

Geneva, 11 May, 2013

Rare 18k yellow-gold chronograph wristwatch with registers and bracelet
Ref. 6265/6263
Case 6250494
Cosmograph Daytona
Oman Coat of Arms
c.1980

CHF 125,000 – 185,000
US$ 133,000 – 196,000

SOLD CHF 155,000

Geneva, 12 November, 2013

Yellow-gold chronograph
wristwatch with registers and
tachymeter
Ref. 6265
Case 5465441
Cosmograph Daytona
c.1977

CHF 35,000 – 45,000
US$ 37,800 – 48,600

SOLD CHF 75,000

1 Geneva, 12 November, 2013

Fine yellow-gold chronograph wristwatch with registers and tachymeter
Ref. 6265/6263
Case 6121127
Cosmograph Daytona
c.1979

CHF 30,000 – 50,000
US$ 32,400 – 54,000

SOLD CHF 40,000

2 Geneva, 14 May, 2014

Yellow-gold chronograph wristwatch with registers and tachymeter
Ref. 6265/6263
Case 8525452
Cosmograph Daytona
c.1982

CHF 30,000 – 50,000
US$ 34,100 – 57,000

SOLD CHF 43,750

3 Geneva, 13 May, 2015

Stainless-steel chronograph wristwatch with bracelet
Ref. 6265
Case 3972513
Cosmograph Daytona
c.1980

CHF 25,000 – 35,000
US$ 25,600 – 35,800

SOLD CHF 31,250

4 New York, 10 December, 2015

Fine stainless-steel chronograph wristwatch with registers and bracelet
Ref. 6265/6263
Case 6043907
Cosmograph Daytona
c.1980

US$ 30,000 – 50,000
€ 26,500 – 44,200
HK$ 233,000 – 388,000

SOLD US$ 37,500

1

2

3

4

London, 25 April, 2017

Stainless-steel chronograph
wristwatch with registers
and bracelet
Ref. 6265/6262
Cosmograph Daytona
'Paul Newman'
'Panda' dial
c.1971

£ 80,000 – 120,000
€ 92,500 – 139,000
US$ 98,000 – 147,000

SOLD £ 272,750

Hong Kong, 2 April, 2018

Rare stainless-steel chronograph
wristwatch with registers, tropical
minute track and bracelet
Ref. 6265
Oyster
Case 3032061
Cosmograph Daytona
'Paul Newman'
c.1972

HK$ 2,000,000 – 4,000,000
US$ 256,000 – 515,000

SOLD HK$ 2,125,000

Geneva, 13 November, 2018

Yellow-gold chronograph
wristwatch with bracelet
Ref. 6265
Cosmograph Daytona
c.1978

CHF 60,000 – 90,000
US$ 61,000 – 91,000

SOLD CHF 93,750

Geneva, 13 November, 2018

Stainless-steel chronograph
wristwatch with bracelet
Ref. 6265
Cosmograph Daytona
'Big Red'
c.1978

CHF 50,000 – 80,000
US$ 50,500 – 81,000

SOLD CHF 106,250

Geneva, 16 November, 2004

Very rare diamond- and sapphire-set gold chronograph wristwatch with registers and bracelet
Ref. 6269
Oyster
Cosmograph Daytona
*c.*1980

CHF 120,000 – 140,000
US$ 98,000 – 147,000

SOLD CHF 138,000

One of the most extraordinary Daytona watches ever made, this example bears the special reference number 6269. Produced in very limited numbers, Ref. 6269 is among the rarest and most impressive chronographs ever manufactured by Rolex.

The dial is encrusted with 240 diamonds and 9 sapphires, a further 44 diamonds are set around the bezel.

Geneva, 13 November, 2018

White-gold chronograph
wristwatch with salmon dial
Ref. 16519
Cosmograph Daytona
'Zenith'
c.1997

CHF 80,000 – 120,000
US$ 81,000 – 122,000

SOLD CHF 150,000

This reference 16519 features the exceedingly rare 'Salmon' dial, which was produced in the late 1990s alongside the mother-of-pearl that usually adorns this reference.

Its 18k white-gold case works in perfect harmony and the combination of colours provides the watch great depth. While it is a shame that the dial failed to make the grade for full production, their scarcity makes them hugely desirable today.

Geneva, 13 May, 2018

Stainless-steel automatic chronograph wristwatch with registers and bracelet
Ref. 16520 MVT 92898
Case W393406
Cosmograph Daytona
'Zenith'
*c.*1995

CHF 10,000 – 15,000
US$ 10,400 – 15,600

SOLD CHF 52,500

The Cosmograph Daytona is now produced entirely in-house, but that was not always the case: before Rolex developed the Calibre 4130, it outsourced the Daytona movement to Zenith.

In 1988, Rolex introduced Ref. 16520, powered by a modified El Primero movement from Zenith.

Ref. 16520 is among the last of the Daytonas to run on a Zenith El Primero movement and is a highly sought-after collector's item.

Hong Kong, 7 October, 2014

Stainless-steel and yellow-gold chronograph wristwatch with registers, diamond-set indexes and bracelet
Ref. 16523
Case A534187
Cosmograph Daytona
c.1999

HK$ 60,000 – 80,000
US$ 7,740 – 10,300

SOLD HK$ 93,750

Before the Rolex Cosmograph Daytona was powered by a Rolex calibre movement, it ran on the Zenith El Primero Calibre 4030 movement, which was modified by Rolex to beat at a rate of 28,800 vph for a smoother reading on or off the race track. A popular collector's item, Ref. 16523 is the two-tone variation of the line, pairing 18-karat yellow-gold with stainless steel.

Geneva, 15 May, 2011

Extremely rare version of the gold and diamond-set automatic chronograph wristwatch
Ref. 16528
Cosmograph Daytona
with dial variant '13'
Letter of confirmation from Rolex
c.1989

CHF 80,000 – 120,000
US$ 88,500 – 133,000

SOLD CHF 122,500

The story of 'The Daytona 13' began in 1989 when a private customer went to the local Rolex retailer to purchase the latest model, Ref. 16528, a gold Cosmograph Daytona.

After a few days he noticed an error on the 15-minutes Arabic indication showing instead the number 13. He immediately wrote to Rolex in Geneva and received a response from its Chairman at the time, Mr. Heinegger, confirming the error on the 15 indication marker. Mr Heinegger also offered the client a replacement of this variant 13 with the normal 15. However, the client had started to enjoy his watch and decided to keep it, which thus became the first 'variant 13' confirmed by Rolex.

New York, 5 December, 2018

White-gold automatic chronograph wristwatch with rubellite and diamond-set dial
Ref. 116519
Cosmograph Daytona
c.2004

US$ 30,000 – 50 ,000
€ 26,300 – 43,800
HK$ 236,000 – 392,000

NOT SOLD

Despite its utilitarian vocation, the legendary sports chronograph was successively released in yellow, white and pink gold. This Daytona example, crafted in white gold, bears a rare rubellite dial. While production quantities of these special watches are unknown, one can assume that they were manufactured in low numbers.

Geneva, 15 May, 2012

Very rare stainless-steel automatic chronograph wristwatch with registers, bracelet and Comex documents
Ref. 116520
Oyster
Cosmograph Daytona
*c.*2002

CHF 15,000 – 25,000
US$ 16,500 – 27,500

SOLD CHF 20,000

In 2000, Rolex debuted the reference 116520, its first Cosmograph Daytona with an in-house movement; previously, the brand had relied on a Zenith movement that they modified to meet their standards. Produced from 2000 until 2016, this particular Rolex reference is sought after by collectors for its incredible history and its wearable style.

Geneva, 14 May, 2014

Very rare stainless-steel automatic chronograph wristwatch with registers, tachymeter and bracelet
Ref. 116520
Case Z479973
Cosmograph Daytona 24 hours
'Race winner'
*c.*2003

CHF 60,000 – 80,000
US$ 68,500 – 91,000

SOLD CHF 75,000

Geneva, 14 May, 2014

Rare diamond- and ruby-set,
white-gold automatic
chronograph wristwatch
with hardstone dial
Ref. 116589/2119
Case K598850
Cosmograph Daytona
*c.*2001

CHF 35,000 – 45,000
US$ 38,800 – 51,500

SOLD CHF 65,000

Geneva, 15 May, 2011

Rare diamond-set, 18k yellow-gold automatic chronograph wristwatch with orange sapphire bezel
Ref. 116598
Cosmograph Daytona
'Leopard'
c.2005

CHF 25,000 – 35,000
US$ 27,700 – 38,700

SOLD CHF 35,000

The Rolex Daytona reference 116598 SACO nicknamed the 'Leopard' was launched at the Basel fair in 2004. Immediately admired for its unconventional appearance, this striking model was destined to be a fashionable hit with collectors and is referred to as a 'wild beauty'.

Geneva, 12 November, 2013

Rare diamond-set, yellow-gold automatic chronograph wristwatch with orange sapphire bezel
Ref. 116598 SACO
Case Z474594
Cosmograph Daytona
'Leopard'
c.2006

CHF 30,000 – 50,000
US$ 32,400 – 54,000

SOLD CHF 52,500

Geneva, 12 November, 2017

Orange sapphire-set, yellow-gold automatic chronograph wristwatch with registers
Ref. 116598 SACO
Case K598540
Cosmograph Daytona
'Leopard'
c.2001

CHF 25,000 – 50,000
US$ 25,700 – 51,500

SOLD CHF 31,250

Geneva, 13 November, 2018

Diamond-set, white-gold
chronograph wristwatch with
mother-of-pearl dial
Ref. 116599
Cosmograph Daytona
c.2001

CHF 50,000 – 70,000
US$ 50,500 – 71,000

SOLD CHF 62,500

New York, 5 December, 2018

Diamond- and ruby-set, white-gold
automatic chronograph wristwatch
with pavé diamond dial
Ref. 116599
Cosmograph Daytona
c.2007

US$ 50,000 – 100,000
€ 43,800 – 87,600

SOLD US$ 68,750

Hong Kong, 2 April, 2018

Rare diamond- and sapphire-set, gold automatic chronograph wristwatch with registers, diamond-set indexes and bracelet
Ref. 116599RBW
Case 9Y557450
Cosmograph Daytona
'Rainbow'
c.2013

HK$ 1,500,000 – 2,500,000
US$ 192,000 – 320,000

SOLD HK$ 2,000,000

The reference 116599RBW first came out in 2012. The most standout feature of the reference 116599RBW is clearly the bezel. Using the classic 18k yellow-gold Cosmograph Daytona case as a base, the bezel is set with multi-coloured baguette-cut sapphires, forming a rainbow to surround the dial. The Rainbow Daytona had an uncommonly short production run for a modern Rolex and is now discontinued. Over its production span, the number of Daytona Rainbows sold was extremely small, hence the availability is extremely limited. This avant-garde creation has slowly grown in the hearts of Rolex collectors and its prices have surged rapidly over the years.

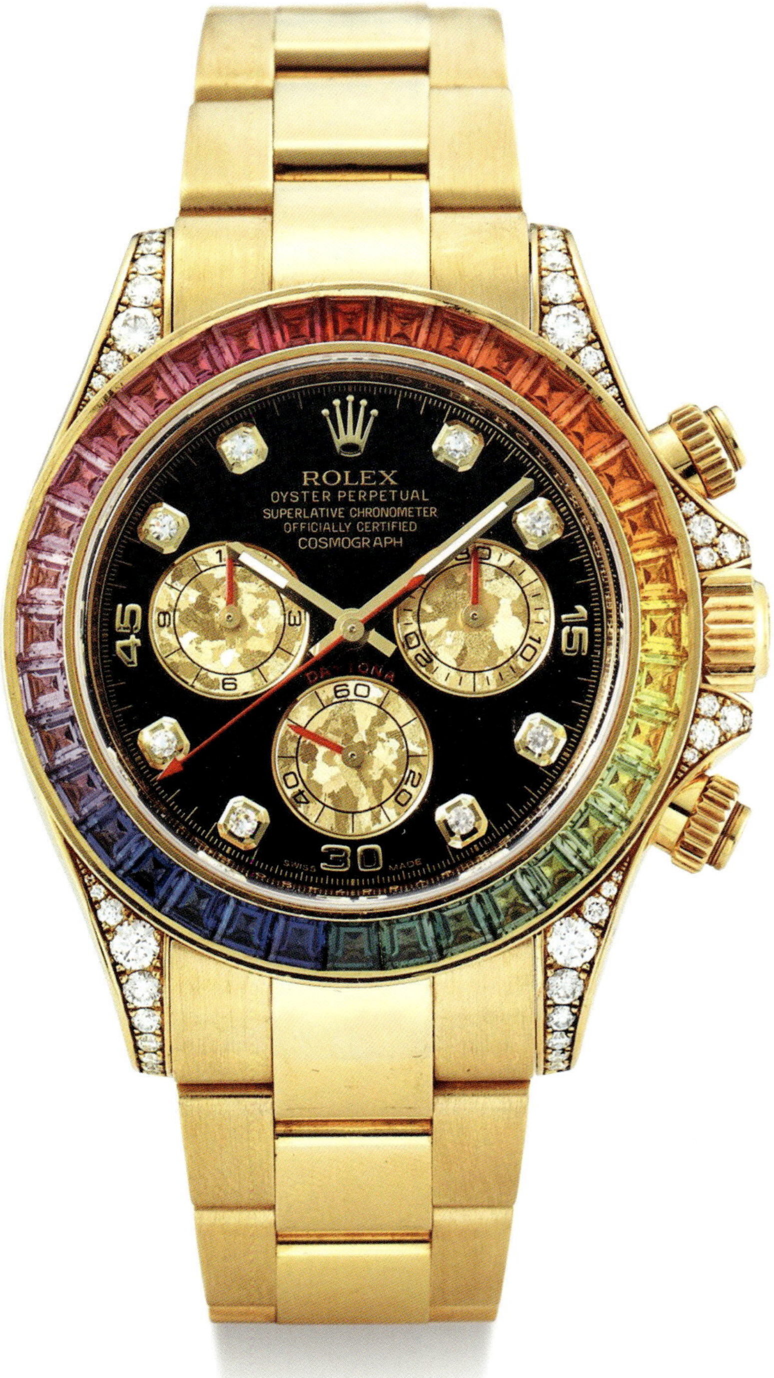

ROLEX
OYSTER PERPETUAL
SUPERLATIVE CHRONOMETER
OFFICIALLY CERTIFIED
COSMOGRAPH

ROLEX
OYSTER PERPETUAL
DATEJUST
18
dallah AVCO
SWISS

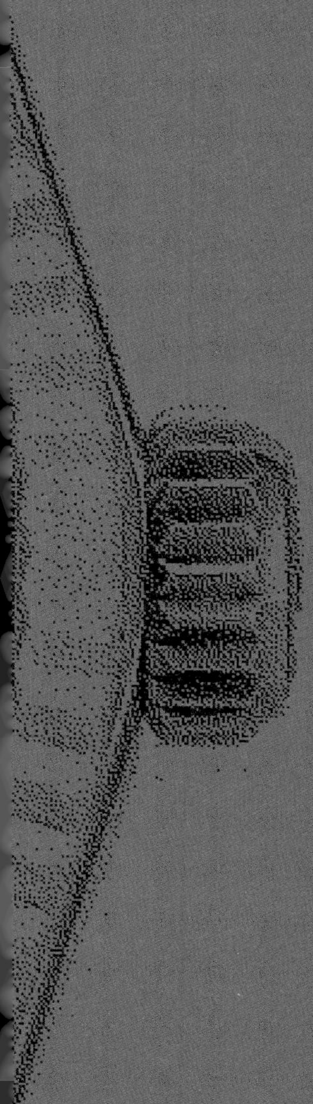

OYSTER PERPETUAL

Geneva, 13 May, 2003

Fine and rare gold automatic sweep-seconds wristwatch with cloisonné enamel map of India Possibly presented to Jawaharlal Nehru, Prime Minister of India, on the occasion of India's first constitutional day of the Republic
Ref. 3372
Oyster Perpetual
*c.*1949

CHF 100,000 – 150,000
US$ 75,000 – 100,000

SOLD CHF 271,200

The bubble-back model was introduced in 1933. Throughout its production, there were countless dial configurations, variations of metal – stainless steel, steel and gold, rose gold, 9k, 10k, 14k, 18k – hooded case variations, even manual wind versions in the 1930s.

The early models through the 1940s featured dials with luminous indexes and luminous hands. Later, in the 1950s, the dials had generally less interesting small raised dial indexes and non-luminous hands.

The date on the dial attests that this watch was most likely a celebratory gift commemorating India's freedom from the British Empire on 26 January, 1950, the first Indian Republic Day. On this date the Constituent Assembly of India came into force, although independence from British rule had been achieved on 15 August, 1947.

Allegedly, Nehru later gave the watch to Tenzing Norgay, the Nepalese mountaineer, during a medal ceremony at India's Presidential Palace honouring the Sherpa's climbing of Mount Everest. Though not this watch, Tenzing Norgay did indeed wear a Rolex on his wrist when he and Sir Edmund Hilary were the first to reach the top of the famed mountain on 29 May 1953.

The current watch came to auction accompanied by a letter from Rolex confirming the watch's manufacture and delivery to Rolex's agent in Bombay in February of 1949. The letter, written to Mr R. Beyer of Chronométrie Beyer Zurich, goes on to state that the watch is possibly one of two examples made for the first Prime Minister, Jawaharlal Nehru, and Babu Rajendra Prasad, the first president of India.

The two watches are very similar. On both watches, the map is considered to be the Indian version, which includes the small corridor of land linking India, Afghanistan and Nepal, and as such was most likely commissioned by a native of India. The 'Nehru' watch is more subdued in colour, the map of India executed in white enamel in a yellow-gold case. The map of 'Prasad' watch, by contrast, is far more vibrant, highlighted by a yellow map of India and pink gold case. Another subtle difference between the two dials is the position of the Rolex signature and crown. The 'Nehru' watch finds the crown just to the left of the hands with the signature below and the date of Indian Independence above. The 'Prasad' watch finds the Rolex signature and crown more

The 'Prasad' watch.

prominently placed at the top of the Indian map. Yet another difference is the style of guilloché executed on each map: the 'Nehru' watch like the 'Prasad' watch is divided into two tones of blue enamel in distinctly different blues, the darker blue representing the countries surrounding India and the lighter blue representing the surrounding sea. The 'Nehru' watch has a guilloché designed as a wavy herringbone motif, while the sea on the 'Prasad' example shows a motif with a far more architectural feel.

Jawaharlal Nehru, Prime Minister of India and Dr Jajendra Prasad, President of India (front row, 5th and 6th from left, respectively) with the members of the Union Cabinet at Government House, New Delhi, 31 January, 1950

Image: Matteo Omeid / Alamy Stock Photo

Geneva, 13 November, 2018

Very rare and attractive pink-gold wristwatch with black laquered dial and bracelet
Ref. 6085
Oyster Perpetual
c.1950

CHF 60,000 – 80,000
US$ 61,000 – 81,000

NOT SOLD

During the 1950s, Rolex produced a variety of time-only wristwatches fitted with very attractive and unusual dials. These watches featured larger case diameters giving the watch much greater presence on the wrist. The present watch, cased in pink gold, is fitted with a black lacquer dial and a pink-gold Rolex brick-link bracelet.

The bottom of the dial is signed 'Swiss', which is correct for a 1950s watch. The amazing black lacquer dial itself has been preserved in excellent condition, having retained its glossy appearance for over sixty years since its manufacture. The case, which has also been retained in excellent condition, features full and robust proportions.

New York, 4 June, 2019

Yellow gold and enamel automatic centre seconds wristwatch with bracelet
Ref. 6290 bombé enamel
Oyster Perpetual
c.1953

US$ 80,000 – 120,000
€ 71,000 – 107,000
HK$ 630,000 – 945,000

NOT SOLD

Produced since the early 1950s, the Rolex 'bombé' is recognised amongst collectors and scholars for its exquisite case design, featuring beautifully crafted inward turned lugs. The present reference 6290 is paired with an exceptional vibrant blue enamel dial manufactured by Stern Frères, further enhancing the watch's rarity.

Bombé models are usually found as reference 6090 and in 14k gold. This reference 6290 in 18k gold is very rare.

1 Dubai, 24 November, 2019

Yellow-gold and stainless-steel wristwatch with date and bracelet
Made for Dallah Avco
Ref. 16013 MVT 0'373'738
Case 7'470'443
Oyster Perpetual Datejust
*c.*1990

US$ 4,000 – 6,000
£ 3,200 – 4,700
AED 14,500 – 22,000

SOLD US$ 3,750

2 Dubai, November 24, 2019

Yellow-gold and stainless-steel wristwatch with date and bracelet
Made for the Sultanate of Oman
Ref. 16013 MVT 1'549'163
Case 9'161'399
Oyster Perpetual Datejust
*c.*1986

US$ 5,000 – 7,000
£ 3,900 – 5,600
AED 18,300 – 25,600

SOLD US$ 5,625

1 Rolex has produced a wide range of models and varieties of watches in its history; special dials fitted on its watches can also be spotted on the market for various reasons and occasions. Founded in 1975, Dallah Avco is an airline company contracted to serve the Saudi Ministry of Defence and Aviation. The present Rolex Datejust is a rare commission from the company, presumably to be given to loyal employees for their dedication; it bears the company signature on the dial. The ref. 16XXX range started to emerge in 1977.

2 Rolexes with the Omani Coat of Arms on the dial are known by collectors as 'Khanjar' and are very collectable today. Rarely seen with 'Royal Khanjar', consisting of a crown placed on top of the Sultanate logo, here stamped in red, this Datejust reference 16013 is, without a doubt, highly collectable.

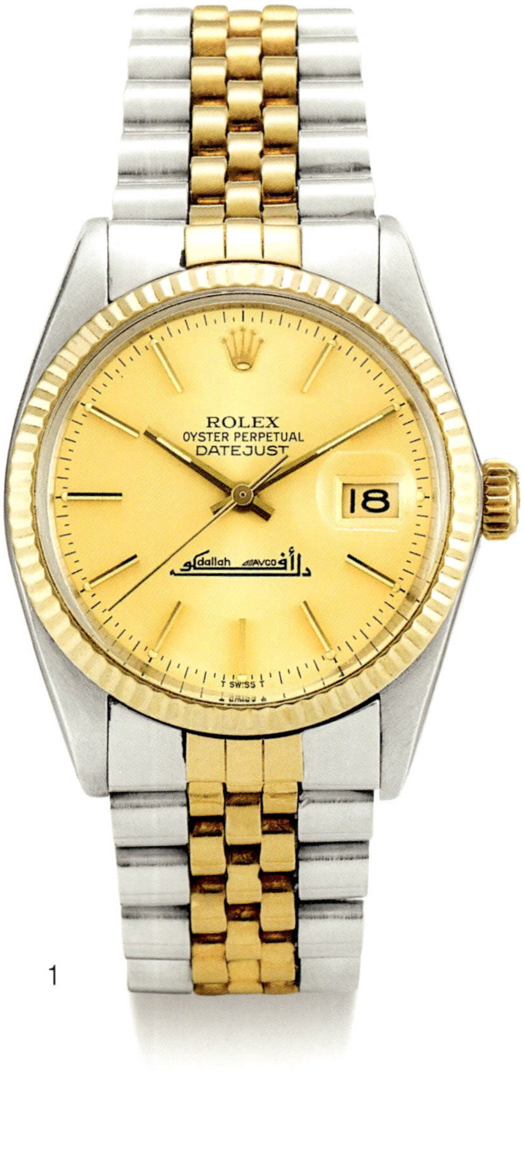

1

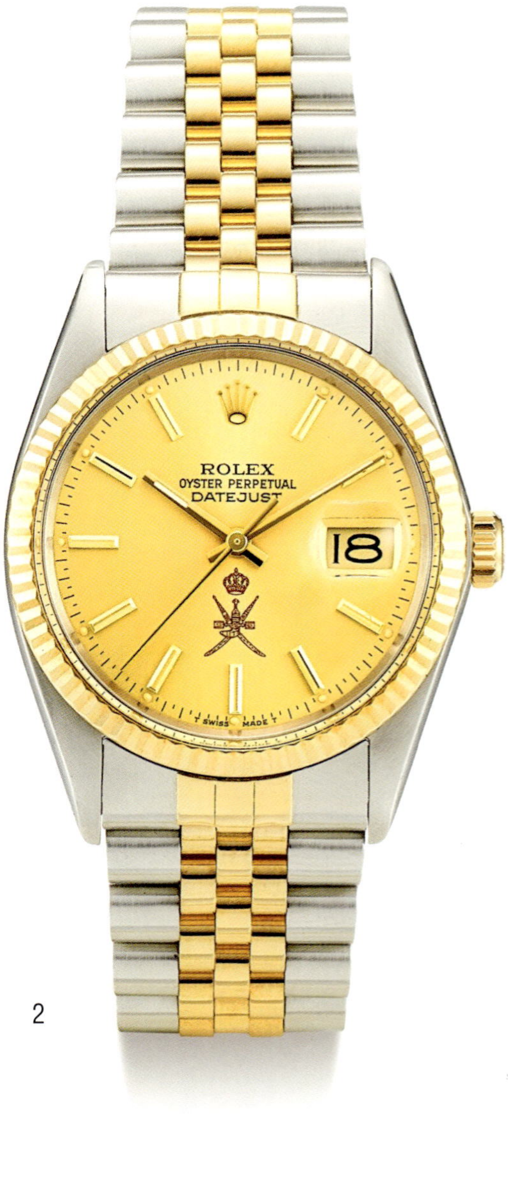

2

Dubai, 24 November, 2019

Diamond- and sapphire-set, yellow-gold wristwatch with bracelet
Ref. 69028
Case 9'710'302
Oyster Perpetual Datejust
c.1986

US$ 30,000 – 50,000
£ 23,700 – 40,000
AED 110,000 – 183,000

NOT SOLD

This is an excellent example of Rolex's quest to create ladies' watches with precious gemstones and diamonds. The present watch is beautifully adorned with sapphire-set hour markers and diamonds throughout the dial, bezel and bracelet. With a total of 458 diamonds, weighing approximately 5.8 carats, this Datejust is a perfect combination of elegance and sophistication.

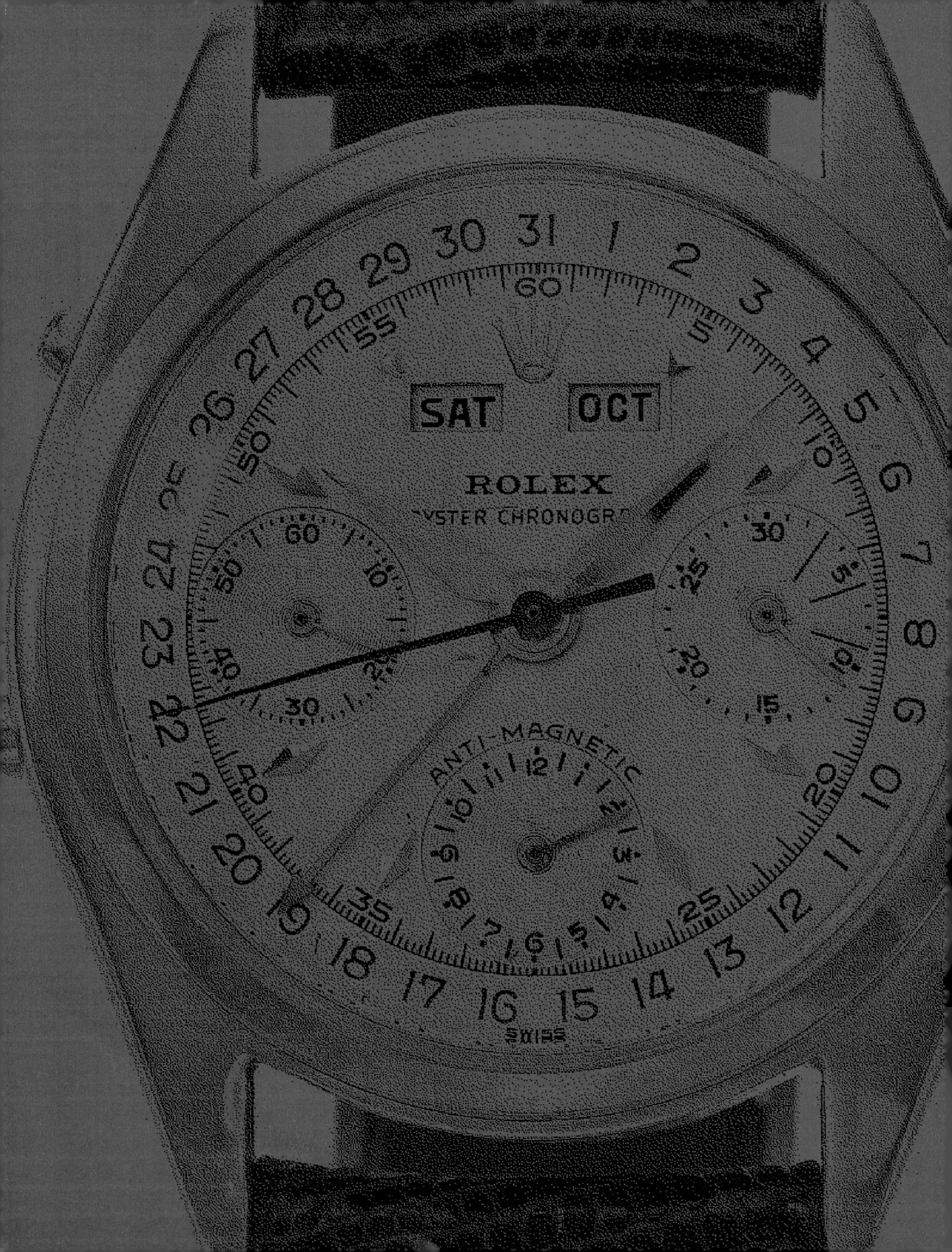
SAT
OCT
ROLEX
ANTI-MAGNETIC
SWISS

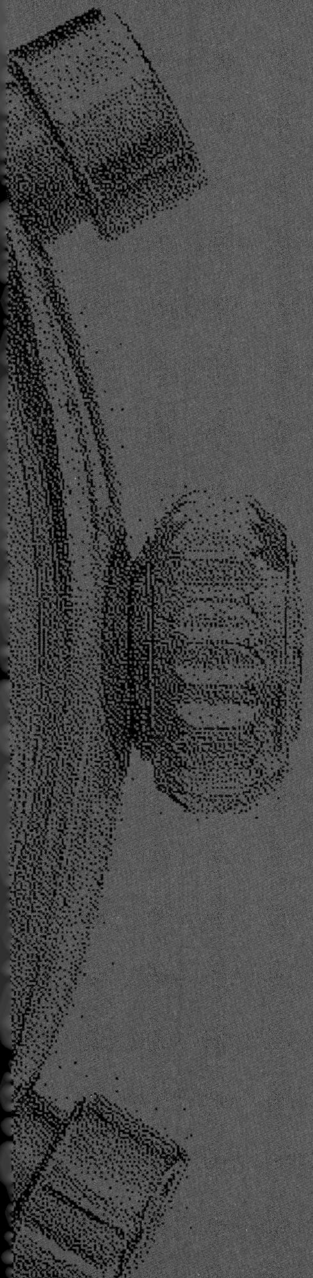

DATO COMPAX

New York, 23 April, 2008

Gold chronograph wristwatch with
triple calendar and registers
Retailed by Serpico y Laino
Ref. 4767
Dato Compax
*c.*1947

US$ 80,000 – 120,000

NOT SOLD

From the mid 1940s to the '60s, Rolex produced 4 references of Oyster anti-magnetic chronograph wristwatches with triple calendar and various dial designs in succession: Ref. 4767, Ref. 5036, Ref. 6036 and Ref. 6236. They became known as 'Jean-Claude Killy', after the French Olympic and World Cup skiing champion.

The reference 4767 was first introduced onto the market in 1947. Made in a very limited series, it was available in yellow and pink gold or stainless steel, with various dial layouts. This reference remains one of the most complicated watches ever made by Rolex, featuring triple calendar and chronograph functions.

Geneva, 16 November, 2008

Rare stainless-steel chronograph wristwatch with triple calendar, registers and bracelet
Ref. 4767
Dato Compax
'Jean-Claude Killy'
*c.*1960

CHF 110,000 – 130,000

NOT SOLD

1 New York, 2 April, 2019

Yellow-gold chronograph wristwatch with triple calendar and registers
Ref. 4767
Dato Compax
*c.*1948

US$ 25,000 – 50,000

NOT SOLD

2 Geneva, 18 June, 2020

Yellow-gold chronograph wristwatch with triple calendar
Ref. 4767
Dato Compax
*c.*1948

CHF 50,000 – 70,000

NOT SOLD

1

2

New York, 5 December, 2005

Rare gold chronograph wristwatch with triple calendar, two-tone dial and registers
Ref. 6036
Case 944073
Oyster
Dato Compax 'Anti-Magnetic'
*c.*1957

US$ 100,000 – 150,000

SOLD US$ 144,000

Rolex produced Ref. 6036 from the mid 1940s to *c.*1957. The dial was continually modified throughout this time, which meant that some examples had very limited productions runs, making them extremely rare now. Our research suggests that approximately 350 pieces were made in yellow gold.

New York, 23 April, 2008

Gold chronograph wristwatch with
triple calendar and registers
Ref. 6036
Dato Compax
'Jean-Claude Killy'
c.1940

US$ 100,000 – 150,000

NOT SOLD

Geneva, 14 November, 2010

Rare 18k pink-gold chronograph
wristwatch with triple calendar
and registers
Retailed by Serpico y Laino
Ref. 6036
Dato Compax
c.1950

CHF 170,000 – 250,000
US$ 174,000 – 255,000

SOLD CHF 206,500

Hong Kong, 6 October, 2011

Rare pink-gold chronograph wristwatch with triple calendar and registers
Retailed by Serpico y Laino
Ref. 6036
Dato Compax
c.1950

HK$ 700,000 – 1,000,000

SOLD HK$ 860,000

New York, 10 December, 2014

Exceptional and very rare yellow-gold anti-magnetic chronograph wristwatch with registers, triple calendar and day and month apertures
Ref. 6036
Case 917831
Dato Compax
'Jean-Claude Killy'
c.1958

US$ 180,000 – 260,000

NOT SOLD

New York, 22 October, 2002

Rare stainless-steel chronograph wristwatch with calendar, registers and bracelet
Ref. 6236
Dato Compax 'Anti-Magnetic'
c.1954

US$ 30,000 – 50,000

SOLD US$ 35,850

Ref. 6236 followed shortly on the heels of a similar Dato-Compax model, Ref. 6036. The main difference between the two models is that the bezel on the later model is a separate third piece, while the earlier version has a two-piece case. The combination of triple calendar and chronograph is especially desirable in today's collector's market. The fact that this model was produced in smaller numbers than other Rolex references makes the series more valuable.

This is one of the most complicated examples that Rolex produced. It is commonly known as the 'Jean-Claude Killy,' after the French Olympic and World Cup skiing champion. It is thought that the first example of this model was presented to Killy, who now sits on the board of Rolex, S.A.

New York, 19 October, 2007

Rare stainless-steel chronograph wristwatch with triple calendar, registers and bracelet
Ref. 6236
Dato Compax 'Anti-Magnetic'
'Jean Claude Killy'
*c.*1958

US$ 80,000 – 120,000

SOLD US$ 109,000

New York, 10 June, 2013

Fine and rare stainless-steel chronograph wristwatch with triple calendar
Ref. 6236
Case 576412
Dato Compax
'Jean Claude Killy'
c.1961

US$ 60,000 – 80,000
€ 46,100 – 61,500
HK$ 466,000 – 625,000

SOLD US$ 161,000

WED
NOV
ROLEX
PERPETUAL
PRECISION

MOONPHASE

New York, 5 December, 2005

Rare automatic gold wristwatch with triple calendar, phases of the moon and two-tone dial
Rolex perpetual
Ref. 8171
Moonphase
c.1957

US$ 40,000 – 50,000

SOLD US$ 78,000

New York, 5 December, 2005

Rare automatic stainless-steel wristwatch with triple calendar, phases of the moon and two-tone dial
Ref. 8171
Rolex perpetual
Moonphase
c.1957

US$ 45,000 – 55,000

SOLD US$ 48,000

New York, 13 June, 2007

Rare automatic gold wristwatch
with triple calendar and phases
of the moon
Ref. 8171
Moonphase
c.1955

US$ 60,000 – 80,000

NOT SOLD

London, 16 July, 2008

Rare automatic stainless-steel wristwatch with triple calendar and phases of the moon
Ref. 8171
Moonphase
*c.*1950

£ 20,000 – 30,000
€ 25,200 – 37,700
US$ 39,600 – 59,500

SOLD £ 73,250

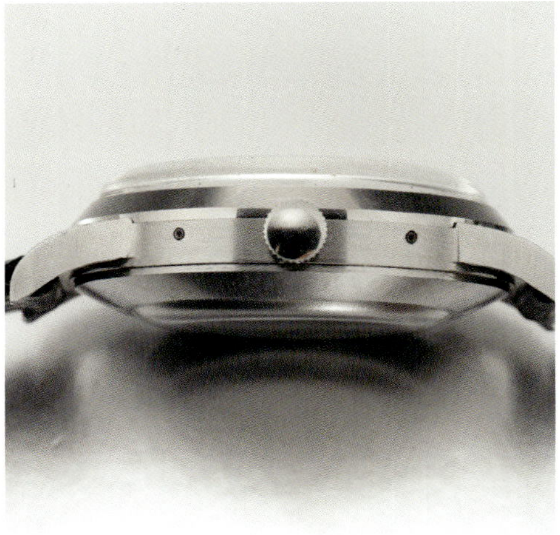

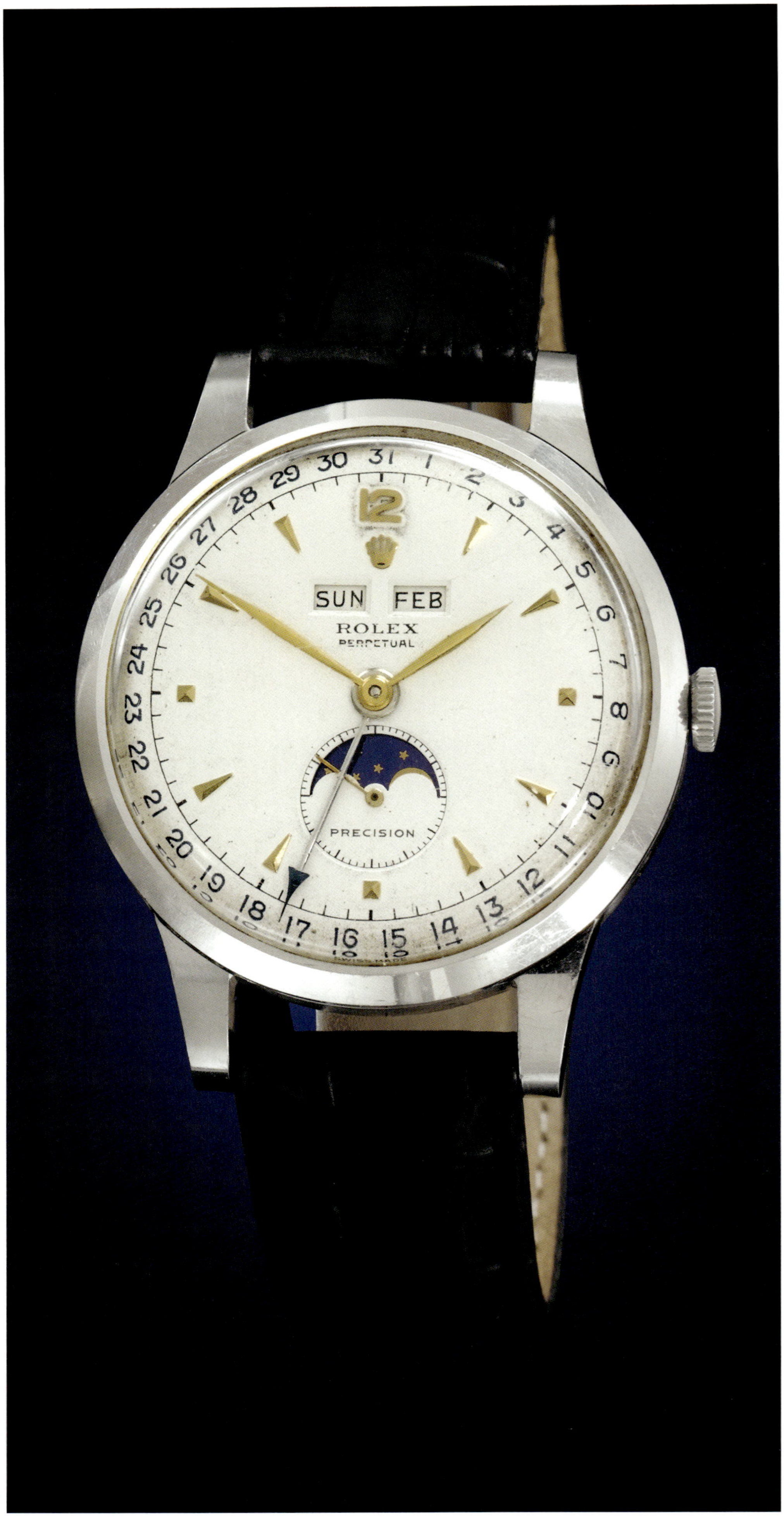

New York, 28 April, 2009

Rare automatic stainless-steel
wristwatch with triple calendar,
phases of the moon and bracelet
Ref. 8171
Moonphase
*c.*1952

US$ 50,000 – 70,000

SOLD US$ 90,100

New York, 5 December, 2018

Automatic stainless-steel wristwatch with triple calendar and phases of the moon
Ref. 8171
Moonphase
'Padellone'
*c.*1952

US$ 100,000 – 200,000
€ 88,000 – 176,000
HK$ 785,000 – 1,570,000

SOLD US$ 387,000

Rolex produced the 8171 for only three years: 1949–1952. Often referred to as the 'Padellone' (Italian for 'frying pan'), this reference is one of the most coveted vintage Rolex watches on the market. At 38 mm, its dial was substantially larger than other models at the time.

Rolex created a name for itself by creating excellent sports watches. As such, triple calendars with moon phases have rarely made an appearance in the firm's history. In fact, Rolex made only two watches with moon phases: Ref. 8171 with the snap-on case back, and Ref. 6062, an Oyster model with a screw-down case back.

New York, 4 June, 2019

Yellow-gold wristwatch with triple calendar and phases of the moon
Ref. 8171
Moonphase
'Padellone'
*c.*1951

US$ 60,000 – 90,000
€ 53,500 – 80,000
HK$ 471,000 – 710,000

SOLD US$ 118,750

1 New York, 26 October, 1999

Rare gold self-winding wristwatch
with calendar and phases of the moon
Ref. 6062
Oyster Perpetual
Moonphase
c.1955

US$ 35,000 – 40,000

SOLD CHF 40,250

2 New York, 26 October, 1999

Rare gold self-winding calendar
wristwatch with phases of the moon
Ref. 6062
Oyster Perpetual
Moonphase
c.1945

US$ 40,000 – 50,000

SOLD US$ 82,250

1

2

3 New York, 6 March, 2002

Rare automatic gold wristwatch
with calendar and phases of the moon
with original *bulletin de marche*
and guarantee
Ref. 6062
Oyster Perpetual
Case 916309
Moonphase
c.1952

US$ 40,000 – 50,000

SOLD US$ 90,450

3

New York, 17 October, 2003

Rare automatic gold wristwatch
with calendar and phases of the moon
Ref. 6062
Oyster Perpetual
Moonphase
c.1950

US$ 30,000 – 35,000

SOLD US$ 36,000

New York, 6 December, 2011

Automatic stainless-steel tonneau
wristwatch with triple calendar and
phases of the moon
Ref. 6062
Case 942644
Moonphase
c.1953

US$ 35,000 – 55,000

SOLD US$ 52,500

Geneva, 15 May, 2012

Exceptional and rare 18k pink-gold wristwatch with triple calendar and phases of the moon
Ref. 6062
Moonphase
'Star dial'
c.1950

CHF 200,000 – 300,000
US$ 220,000 – 330,000

SOLD CHF 314,500

The attractive and unusual 'Star Dial' or 'Stelline Dial' was the launch version of Ref. 6062 in 1950. Only very few Rolex watches bearing the Ref. 6062 have been recorded; research suggests that about 180 pieces were made.

Ref. 6062 is one of only two models that Rolex produced with date, week days, month and moonphase indication.

ROLEX
OYSTER PERPETUAL
FRI
OCT
OFFICIALLY CERTIFIED
CHRONOMETER
SWISS

Geneva, 12 November, 2013

Rare automatic yellow-gold wristwatch with triple calendar and phases of the moon
Ref. 6062
Case 911131
Moonphase
'Star dial'
*c.*1952

CHF 80,000 – 120,000

NOT SOLD

Geneva, 14 May, 2014

Rare automatic yellow-gold
wristwatch with triple calendar
and phases of the moon
Ref. 6062
Case 916361
Moonphase
'Star dial'
c.1952

CHF 80,000 – 160,000
US$ 91,000 – 182,000

SOLD CHF 209,000

200m = 660ft
SUBMARINER
SWISS

SUBMARINER

New York, 23 April, 2008

Rare automatic stainless-steel wristwatch with sweep seconds and bracelet
Ref. 6200
Oyster Perpetual Submariner
'Big Crown James Bond'
*c.*1955

US$ 80,000 – 120,000

SOLD US$ 115,000

Ref. 6200 was the first Submariner model that Rolex produced. Launched in the early 1950s, it was initially rated for a depth of 200m, or 660ft. The model is most clearly defined by its unusual dial – sometimes called an 'Explorer' dial – with Arabic 3, 6 and 9 and wider triangle at 12 o'clock.

The watch features a thicker profile compared to other Submariner models of the same period, a domed back to account for the movement's rotor and a rotating bezel calibrated for 60 units.

This example is rather unusual in that it features the word 'Submariner', which was not normally printed on dials of this reference. The model name was not standardised until the subsequent model, Ref. 6204. The dial on this example is also signed 'Officially Certified Chronometer', which is another unusual feature not normally seen on this model.

The present example features a bezel that was most likely intended for a Milgauss, Ref. 6541, and gilt hands that were probably intended for a Submariner, Ref. 6536. It can be assumed that these parts were changed during a service at some point after the original sale.

Geneva, 13 November, 2012

Rare automatic stainless-steel diver's wristwatch with centre seconds and bracelet
Ref. 6536/1
Case 112229
Submariner
'Red Depth'
c.1955

CHF 10,000 – 15,000
US$ 10,700 – 16,100

SOLD CHF 20,000

Pre-dating the introduction of crown guards, the 6536 is characterised by its thinner profile and small crown; it is recognised as a transitional reference between the earliest examples and the 'Big Crown' references.

Ref. 6536/1 was an improvement on its predecessor, the Ref. 6536, as it featured a chronometer-grade cal. 1030 movement. This example of a Ref. 6536/1 is among the most sought after Submariner models, featuring the very first depth rating used by Rolex, 100/330 printed in red. This style of printing is known to exist on only a very small series of this reference, on all later models the more common 100m=330ft was printed in white on Submariner models.

Geneva, 12 November, 2013

Automatic stainless-steel
diver's wristwatch with centre
seconds and bracelet
Ref. 6536/1
Case 229990
Submariner
'Tropical dial'
c.1957

CHF 6,000 – 10,000
US$ 6,500 – 10,800

SOLD CHF 7,500

New York, 19 October, 2007

Rare automatic stainless-steel wristwatch with sweep seconds and bracelet
Ref. 6538
Oyster Perpetual
Submariner
'Big Crown James Bond'
c.1959

US$ 35,000 – 45,000

SOLD US$ 85,000

By the time that Ref. 6538, was released in the late 1950s, Rolex had settled on its design for the Submariner. The depth rating for the watch would be printed on the dial above 6 o'clock, along with the word 'Submariner', which was finally standardised around the same time. It would also have a rotating black bezel that could be used by divers for timing their oxygen reserve, as well as a screw-down crown that would allow the watch to withstand the pressures of underwater use. When the Ref. 6538 replaced the older 6204, it was further rated to a depth of 660 feet or roughly 200 metres. It would also have a thicker case than its predecessor.

The most significant design feature of this model is the large crown with no crown guard shoulders. Now known to collectors as the 'Big Crown James Bond,' this model is especially rare, as by the end of the 1950s Rolex replaced the large crown design (8mm diameter) with a smaller one (6mm diameter). For this reason, the larger crown with the word 'Brevet' commands more attention and more value in today's collecting world.

The nickname 'James Bond' comes from the fact that Submariner models without crown guards were frequently used in the Bond movies. In fact, it is likely that the Submariner used in some of the early Bond films, including *Dr. No*, *Goldfinger* and *You Only Live Twice*, were examples of this model, Ref. 6538. Today any Submariner without crown guards, regardless of the reference or year of production, is referred to as a 'James Bond'.

New York, 23 April, 2008

Rare automatic stainless-steel
wristwatch with sweep seconds
Ref. 6538
Oyster Perpetual
Submariner
'Big Crown James Bond'
c.1959

US$ 60,000 – 80,000

SOLD US$ 211,000

This example of a second-generation Ref. 6538, shows the phrase 'Officially Certified Chronometer' below the word 'Submariner'. It is interesting to note that the earlier generation Ref. 6538 featured the same movement, but was not designated as such on the dial. This expanded signature is commonly known as the 'four-line' dial and is highly collectible. The beautiful chocolate-tone dial on the present watch makes it even more rare and interesting to collectors.

Geneva, 16 November, 2008

Rare automatic stainless-steel
wristwatch with centre seconds
Ref. 6538
Oyster Perpetual
Submariner
'Big Crown James Bond'
c.1957

CHF 50,000 – 70,000
US$ 44,800 – 63,000

SOLD CHF 55,000

Geneva, 15 May, 2011

Rare automatic stainless-steel wristwatch with centre seconds and bracelet
Retailed by Tiffany and Co.
Ref. 6538
Oyster Perpetual
Submariner
'Big Crown James Bond'
c.1958

CHF 85,000 – 95,000
US$ 94,000 – 105,000

SOLD CHF 104,500

Geneva, 12 November, 2013

Rare stainless-steel diver's wristwatch with centre seconds
Ref. 6538
Case 140246
Oyster Perpetual
Submariner
'Big Crown James Bond'
c.1956

CHF 20,000 – 30,000
US$ 21,600 – 32,400

SOLD CHF 25,000

London, 25 September, 2018

Very rare stainless-steel wristwatch with centre seconds, tropical dial and bracelet
Ref. 6538
Case 448969
Submariner
'Big Crown'
*c.*1959

£ 70,000 – 120,000
€ 78,500 – 135,000
US$ 91,000 – 156,000

SOLD £ 274,000

Geneva, 12 November, 2019

Stainless-steel wristwatch with tropical dial and bracelet
Ref. 6538 MVT DN'775'122
Case 426'315
Submariner
'Big Crown'
c.1958

CHF 150,000 – 300,000
US$ 151,000 – 302,000

NOT SOLD

Geneva, 14 May, 2014

Automatic stainless-steel diver's wristwatch with centre seconds
Ref. 5508
Submariner
100m = 330ft
c.1962

CHF 30,000 – 50,000
US$ 34,100 – 57,000

SOLD CHF 155,000

Reference 5508 was produced between 1957 and 1961. The dial combines gilt printing with the depth rating in white, creating an attractive contrast. This reference was the last Submariner not to have crown guards. It is also known as the 'James Bond' Submariner thanks to its appearance on the wrist of the famous ficticious British spy.

New York, 24 May, 2018

Automatic stainless-steel
wristwatch with centre seconds
Ref. 5508
Submariner
'Small Crown James Bond'
c.1960

US$ 12,000 – 18,000
€ 9,800 – 14,700
HK$ 94,500 – 142,000

SOLD US$ 17,500

Geneva, 12 November, 2019

Stainless-steel wristwatch
with bracelet
Ref. 5508 MVT 19'448
Case 361'469
Submariner
'Small Crown James Bond'
c.1958

CHF 30,000 – 50,000
US$ 30,200 – 50,500

SOLD CHF 41,250

New York, 17 October, 2008

Automatic stainless-steel
wristwatch with sweep seconds
and bracelet
Ref. 5510
Submariner
'Big Crown James Bond'
c.1951

US$ 30,000 – 50,000

SOLD US$ 43,750

Only produced during a very short period, this 'James Bond' watch is easily identified by its big 'Brevet' crown, the absence of crown guards, and the bezel with a red triangle.

Known to collectors as the 'Big Crown James Bond' or 'coroncione' ('big crown' in Italian), this model is especially rare, as Rolex would replace the large crown (8mm in diameter) with a smaller one (5 or 6 mm) by the end of the 1950s.

Geneva, 15 May, 2011

Rare automatic stainless-steel wristwatch with centre seconds and bracelet
Ref. 5510
Submariner
'Big Crown James Bond'
*c.*1958

CHF 30,000 – 50,000
US$ 33,200 – 55,500

SOLD CHF 37,500

New York, 17 October, 2008

Automatic stainless-steel
wristwatch with sweep seconds
and bracelet
Ref. 5512
Submariner
'Point Crown Guards'
c.1962

US$ 20,000 – 30,000

SOLD US$ 30,000

This example belongs to the second series of the 5512 reference.

Geneva, 13 November, 2012

Rare automatic stainless-steel
diver's wristwatch with centre
seconds and bracelet
Ref. 5512
Case 477948
Submariner
200m = 660ft
'Square Crown Guards'
c.1959

CHF 25,000 – 35,000
US$ 26,700 – 37,400

SOLD CHF 74,500

Geneva, 12 November, 2013

Rare automatic stainless-steel diver's wristwatch with centre seconds
Ref. 5512
Case 478007
Submariner 200m = 660ft
'Square Crown Guards'
c.1959

CHF 25,000 – 35,000
US$ 27,000 – 37,800

SOLD CHF 52,500

Reference 5512 was introduced in 1959 as the first Submariner model to feature the now iconic protective crown guard case. The early models (to which this model belongs) are very rare to find because of the few examples made. They were produced with square-ended crown guards and fitted with a gloss black dial. The second generation features a chronometer grade calibre, and is further identified by the fine gilt and silvered four line print on the dial for depth measure and chronometer certification. The second series also features pointed crown guards.

Geneva, 14 May, 2014

Automatic stainless-steel diver's wristwatch with centre seconds and bracelet
Ref. 5512
Case 1781495
Submariner 200m=660ft
c.1966

CHF 20,000 – 30,000
US$ 20,800 – 34,100

SOLD CHF 25,000

Geneva, 16 November, 2004

Rare automatic stainless-steel wristwatch with centre seconds and Explorer-style dial
Ref. 5513
Oyster Perpetual
Submariner
c.1967

CHF 12,000 – 15,000
US$ 9,600 – 11,900

SOLD CHF 26,400

Reference 5513 was introduced in 1962 and remained in production until 1989.

Widely considered the pinnacle model in the Rolex Submariner lineage, it features the rare and incredibly sought after 'Explorer' type dial. Fitted only to watches manufactured during the first four or five years of production, it combines traditional baton indexes with the addition of the Arabic numerals at 3, 6 and 9.

Geneva, 16 November, 2008

Rare automatic stainless-steel wristwatch with centre seconds
Ref. 5513
Oyster Perpetual Submariner
Made for the British Royal Navy
*c.*1972

CHF 50,000 – 70,000
US$ 44,800 – 63,000

SOLD CHF 53,750

The reference 5513 became an official Military issue model after the British Royal Navy commissioned a series of Submariners with specific adaptations. The Military Submariner Ref. 5513 was either delivered with sword hands or mercedes-style hands, both with the diamond tip seconds (these configurations are unique to this model). The strap bars of the watch were soldered in place so that they could only be fitted with a non-reflective cloth strap. The dial was marked with an encircled 'T' to indicate the use of the luminous material tritium. The watches were also fitted with the hacking feature (stop-seconds function), which was only introduced on the chronometer models at a later date and allowed the easy synchronisation of time, an especially useful function for troops on operations.

London, 18 December, 2008

Rare automatic stainless-steel
wristwatch with centre seconds
Ref. 5513
Oyster Perpetual Submariner
Made for the British Royal Navy
c.1974

£ 30,000 – 50,000
€ 37,600 – 63,000
US$ 46,700 – 78,000

SOLD £ 27,500

Geneva, 11 May, 2013

Rare military issue automatic
stainless-steel wristwatch with
centre seconds
Ref. 5513
Case 3764824
Submariner
c.1974

CHF 45,000 – 65,000
US$ 47,700 – 69,000

SOLD CHF 52,500

1 Geneva, 11 May, 2013

Rare military issue automatic stainless-steel wristwatch with centre seconds
Ref. 5513
Case 3927016
Submariner
c.1972

CHF 40,000 – 60,000
US$ 42,400 – 64,000

SOLD CHF 50,000

1

2 Geneva, 12 November, 2013

Military issue automatic stainless-steel wristwatch with centre seconds
Ref. 5513
Case 3926860
Submariner
c.1975

CHF 12,000 – 18,000
US$ 13,000 – 19,500

SOLD CHF 37,500

2

3 Geneva, 14 May, 2016

Rare military issue automatic stainless-steel diver's wristwatch with centre seconds
Ref. 5513
Case 2940830
Submariner
660ft = 200m
c.1972

CHF 25,000 – 35,000
US$ 25,700 – 36,000

SOLD CHF 41,250

3

Hong Kong, 2 April, 2018

Exceptionally rare automatic stainless-steel wristwatch with 'underlined' Explorer gilt dial, centre seconds, pointed crown guards and bracelet
Ref. 5513
Case 1009589
Submariner
Explorer dial
c.1963

HK$ 1,200,000 – 2,400,000
US$ 154,000 – 307,000

SOLD HK$ 1,750,000

This particular example has been marked with an 'underline' to the dial beneath the signature at 12 o'clock. One theory is that this underline denotes the transition period between the use of radium luminescence and tritium luminescence. Indeed, measurements have been taken showing that these 'underline' dials emit lower levels of radiation suggesting the presence of tritium rather than radium.

London, 17 April, 2018

Automatic stainless-steel diver's watch with Explorer dial and centre seconds
Ref. 5513
Case 1170505
Submariner
c.1964

£ 30,000 – 50,000
US$ 34,200 – 57,000

SOLD £ 75,000

Geneva, 13 November, 2018

Stainless-steel wristwatch with underline dial and pointed crown guards
Ref. 5513
Submariner
c.1963

CHF 40,000 – 60,000
US$ 40,400 – 61,000

SOLD CHF 50,000

Geneva, 12 November, 2019

Stainless-steel wristwatch and bracelet
Ref. 5513
Case L'649'260
Submariner
c.1988

CHF 8,000 – 12,000
US$ 8,100 – 12,100

SOLD CHF 10,000

London, 16 July, 2008

Very rare automatic stainless-steel diver's wristwatch with bracelet
Ref. 5513/5514
Oyster Perpetual
Submariner Comex
c.1972

£ 25,000 – 35,000
€ 31,400 – 44,000
US$ 49,500 – 69,500

SOLD £ 31,250

London, 18 December, 2008

Very rare automatic stainless-steel diver's wristwatch with bracelet
Ref. 5513/5514
Oyster Perpetual
Submariner Comex
c.1977

£ 40,000 – 60,000
€ 50,500 – 75,500
US$ 62,500 – 93,500

SOLD £ 28,000

Geneva, 13 May, 2018

Very rare automatic stainless-steel diver's wristwatch with bracelet
Ref. 5514
Oyster Perpetual
Submariner Comex
c.1977

CHF 30,000 – 50,000
US$ 29,100 – 48,000

SOLD CHF 68,000

Comex (Compagnie Maritime d'Expertise) was founded in Marseille in 1961, at a time when industrial deep-sea diving did not yet exist. Very soon, however, Comex promoted new technology and became a pioneer in deep diving operations for the offshore oil industry; today, the company has over 2,000 employees and 800 divers located all over the world.

At the end of the 1960s, Comex asked Rolex to create a watch that could withstand high pressure in deep waters as the compressed and saturated air began causing a build-up of pressure in the standard Submariner case, destroying its mechanism. Rolex rapidly came up with a patented solution by installing a one-way pressure relief valve on the side of the watch case, beside the 9 o'clock position, that allowed the release of helium from the case. Initially, this gas escape valve was featured on special Reference 5513 models, however, the model was then re-named Reference 5514.

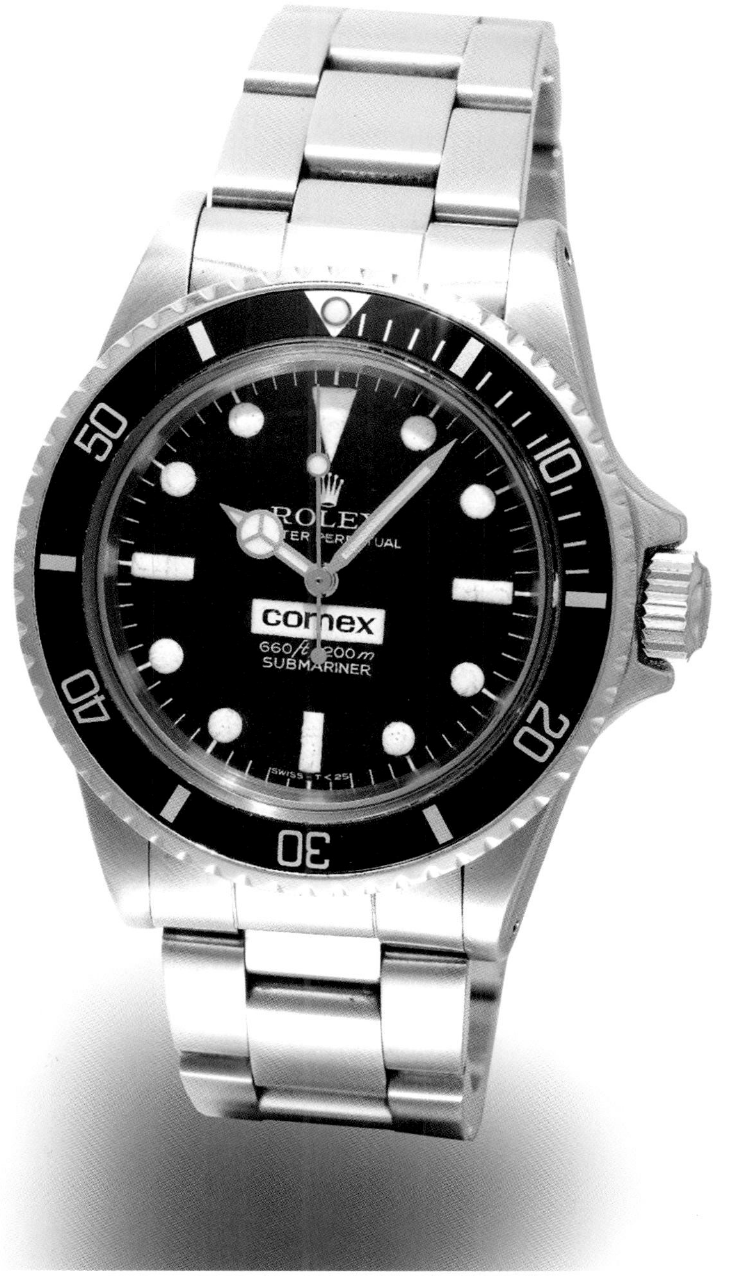

London, 16 July, 2008

Rare automatic stainless-steel wristwatch with centre seconds
Ref. 5513/5517
Oyster Perpetual Submariner
Made for the British Royal Navy
c.1972

£ 25,000 – 35,000
€ 31,400 – 44,000
US$ 49,500 – 69,500

SOLD £ 70,850

The reference 5517 is a special military example made for the Special Boat Service of the Royal Marines in the 1970s. Reference 5517/5513 had all the characteristic of its predecessor, reference 5513, but was especially ordered from Rolex by the Royal Navy for use by the commandos of the British Special Boat Service, one of the world's most highly trained Special Forces. All inside case backs were engraved on the interior with the serial number to avoid backs being swapped during servicing.

Geneva, 13 November, 2018

Military issue stainless-steel
wristwatch
Made for the British Armed Forces
Ref. 5517
Submariner 'Milsub'
c.1978

CHF 150,000 – 300,000
US$ 152,000 – 303,000

SOLD CHF 218,750

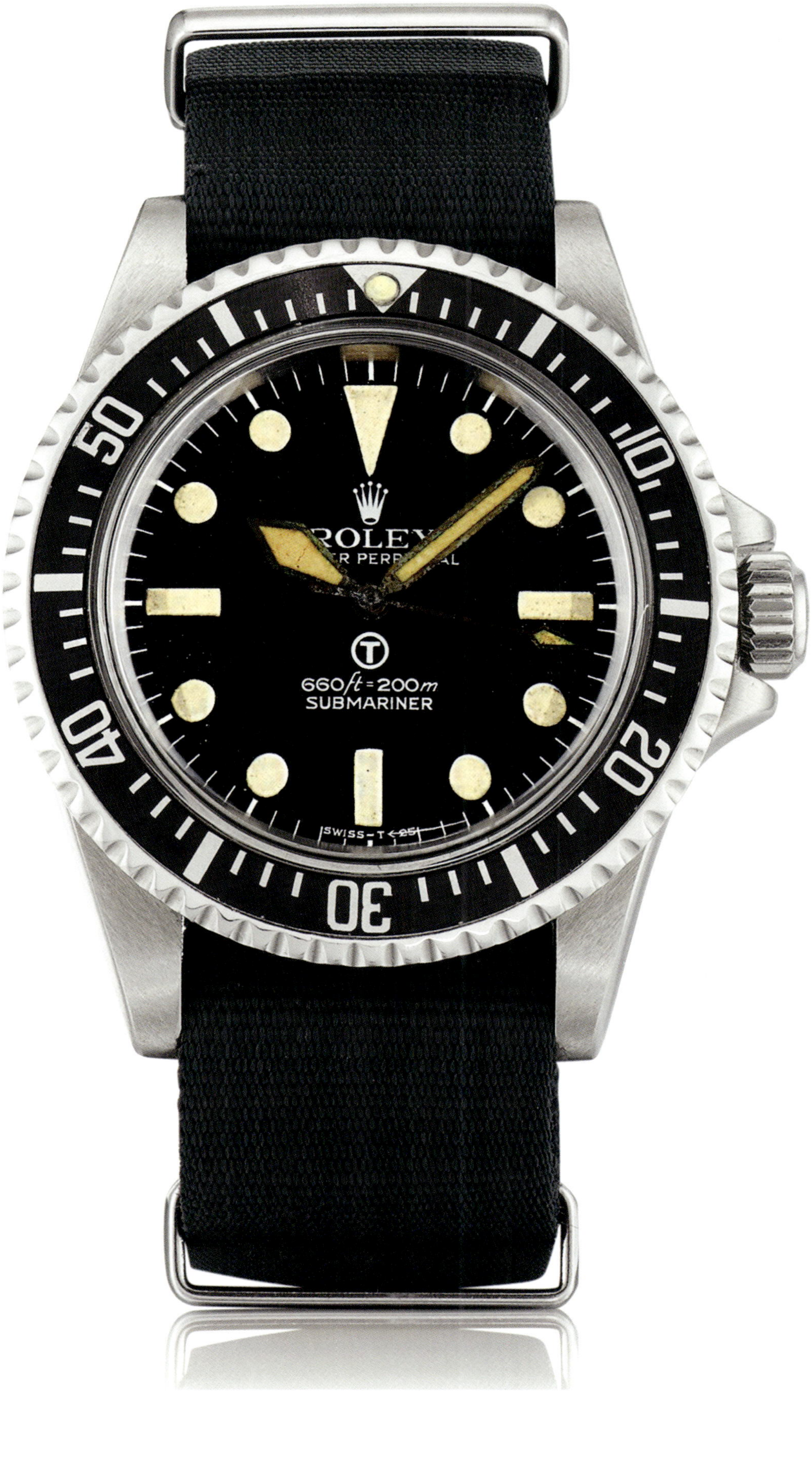

Hong Kong, 2 April, 2004

Automatic stainless-steel wristwatch with date, centre seconds and bracelet
Made for the Peruvian Airforce
Ref. 1680
Case 3715664
Submariner Single Red
c.1977

HK$ 160,000 – 240,000
US$ 20,500 – 30,700

SOLD HK$ 400,000

An extremely important reference in the Submariner history, Ref. 1680 was released in 1967 and produced until 1978. The new model brought with it the calibre 1575, which finally featured the anticipated addition of a date display, a convenient complication achieved by adding a date module to the trustworthy calibre 1570. Furthermore, the reference 1680 was waterproof up to 200 metres. Examples from this reference can be split into two main categories, cosmetically differentiated by their dial: watches produced until 1976 bear a red Submariner script, while later examples bear only white text (with feet-first depth indication) on their dial.

One of the most significant changes that the Submariner saw over the years, was the introduction of a date window with a cyclops for certain references. This change was first put in place on the reference 1680.

Geneva, 14 May, 2014

Automatic stainless-steel diver's wristwatch with date, centre seconds and bracelet
Ref. 1680
Case 5287744
Submariner
660ft = 200m
c.1977

CHF 10,000 – 15,000
US$ 11,400 – 17,100

SOLD CHF 12,500

1 Geneva, 13 November, 2018

Yellow-gold wristwatch with date and colour changed nipple dial
Ref. 1680
Submariner
c.1969

CHF 20,000 – 30,000
US$ 20,200 – 30,300

SOLD CHF 45,000

1

2 Geneva, 13 November, 2018

Stainless-steel wristwatch with date and bracelet
Made for Hafez AL Assad
Ref. 1680
Submariner
c.1968

CHF 120,000 – 180,000
US$ 122,000 – 182,000

NOT SOLD

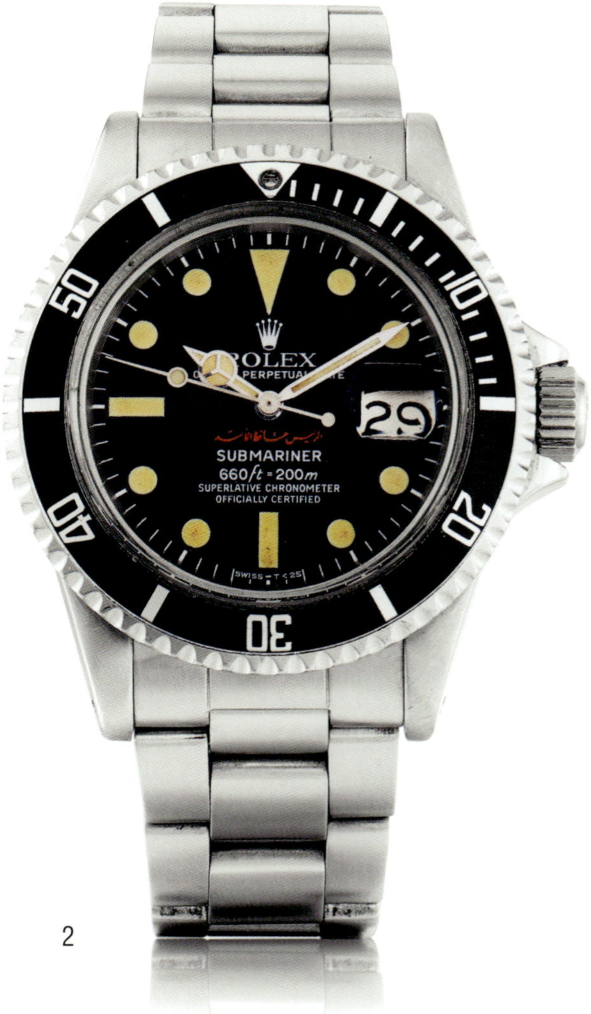

2

Geneva, 14 May, 2014

Automatic stainless-steel diver's wristwatch with date, centre seconds and bracelet
Ref. 16800
Case 8680523
Submariner
1000ft = 300m
c.1984

CHF 6,000 – 10 ,000
US$ 6,900 – 11,400

SOLD CHF 7,500

Rolex introduced the reference 16800 in 1978, replacing the 1680. This brought with it several changes, some more noticeable than others. Rolex re-designed the case in order to increase the depth rating from 200 metres (660 feet) to 300 metres (1,000 feet). This was also the first Submariner to be fitted with the Rolex calibre 3035, which not only runs at a higher frequency than the previous calibre 1570, but it also features the very practical quickset date function, which means the date can be set separately to setting the time, making it more user friendly. Other features introduced with this reference, and still used today, were the sapphire crystal, which offers increased scratch resistance compared to acrylic crystal and a uni-directional bezel. The uni-directional bezel is a useful safety feature for divers, as it prevents the bezel from being turned anti-clockwise, and thus accidentally misleading the diver about their remaining oxygen time.

New York, 17 October, 2008

Rare automatic stainless-steel wristwatch with sweep seconds, date and bracelet
Ref. 16610
Submariner Comex
c.1997

US$ 80,000 – 120,000

NOT SOLD

The reference 16610 – produced for more than 20 years between 1987 and 2010 – introduced major technical innovations. It replaced the outgoing Submariner reference 16800 and is considered by many collectors as the last 'pre-modern' iteration, before Rolex introduced the maxi cases and the ceramic bezel insert with Ref. 116610.

New York, 11 December, 2019

Automatic stainless-steel wristwatch with date and bracelet
Ref. 16610T 'Kermit' MVT 31595778
Case Z999160
Submariner
c.2006

US$ 10,000 – 15,000
€ 7,200 – 10,800
HK$ 63,000 – 94,500

SOLD US$ 13,750

London, 25 September, 2018

Rare automatic yellow-gold wristwatch with lapis lazuli dial, centre seconds, date and bracelet
Ref. 16618
Case X706579
Submariner
c.1991

£ 30,000 – 50,000
€ 33,600 – 56,000
US$ 38,900 – 65,000

SOLD £ 43,750

The reference 16618 Submariner was in production from 1988 to 2008.

Over its lifespan, numerous dial and bezel colours were introduced, including a black dial, champagne dial, and also diamond- or sapphire-set indexes. Without a doubt, examples of Ref. 16618 with lapis lazuli or onyx dials should be considered the rarest as only a handful of them were produced during the early 1990s.

The present example is equipped with a lapis lazuli dial, showcasing a striking ultramarine blue tone. It is extremely difficult to manufacture dials with lapis lazuli due to the delicate nature of the material, and it also took arduous work to carve the stone to appropriate sizing.

A Ref. 16618 with lapis lazuli dial is not only a rare and highly collectible piece, it is also considered by many enthusiasts as the most beautiful version of the gold Submariner.

Geneva, 13 May, 2015

Rare and special order automatic stainless-steel wristwatch with centre seconds, date and bracelet
Made for the Special Reconnaissance Regiment
Ref 116610
Case 48w5k742
Submariner
1000ft=300m
c.2013

CHF 15,000 – 25,000

SOLD 43,750 CHF

Since its introduction in 1953, the Rolex Submariner was continuously upgraded and saw many technical evolutions. Superseding the 16610, the reference 116610 was introduced in a stainless-steel and gold combination in 2009, unveiling to the market the face of the 'modern Submariner'.

In 2010, Rolex released the highly anticipated stainless-steel version of the world's most famous diver's watch.

This watch is one of 66, of a special order supplied directly to the Special Reconnaissance Regiment by Rolex. The certificate, issued by the Regiment, gives the serial number of the watch and its limited edition number (in this case, No. 403), which is also engraved on the back of the watch.

The Special Reconnaissance Regiment (SRR), a Special Forces Regiment of the British Armed Forces, was established in 2005 to meet the demand for special reconnaissance capability. The regiment conducts a wide range of classified activities related to covert surveillance and reconnaissance. It is believed to comprise no more than 100–300 personnel.

Hong Kong, 3 April, 2019

Limited edition diamond- and emerald-set white-gold wristwatch with date and bracelet
Ref. 116649 EM
Submariner Emerald
c.2010

HK$ 1,600,000 – 2,700,000
US$ 204,000 – 319,000

SOLD HK$ 2,187,500

At the 2010 Basel World, Rolex introduced its extremely rare and limited Rolex Submariner (Ref. 116649EM). Nicknamed the 'Submariner Emerald', it includes 36 emeralds and 12 diamonds on the bezel, a pavé-set diamond dial with 8 emerald-set hour markers and comes complete with a part pavé-set diamond bracelet.

50
40
30
TURN-O-GRAPH

TURN-O-GRAPH

New York, 10 June, 2013

Automatic stainless-steel
wristwatch with centre seconds
Ref. 6202
Case 949375
Turn-o-graph
*c.*1954

US$ 5,000 – 7,000

SOLD US$ 6,250

London, 22 September, 2015

Rare automatic stainless-steel wristwatch with centre seconds and bracelet
Ref. 6202
Case 952360
Turn-o-graph
*c.*1954

£ 5,000 – 8,000
€ 7,200 – 11,400
US$ 7,800 – 12,500

SOLD £ 11,500

Ref. 6202 was released and first presented at the Basel Fair in 1953.

The Turn-O-Graph was the first series-produced Rolex to feature a rotating bezel. Rolex often promoted this first series tool watch as a convenient and simple way of calculating the 'timing of a transatlantic telephone call, the rate of a machine, a patient's pulse or the speed of a train.' The model was ultimately pulled from production in the early 1960s.

Geneva, 14 May, 2017

Automatic stainless-steel
wristwatch with centre seconds
and bracelet
Ref. 6202
Turn-o-graph
c.1954

CHF 4,800 – 6,800

SOLD CHF 9,375

New York, 7 June, 2017

Rare automatic stainless-steel
wristwatch with centre seconds
and bracelet
Ref. 6202 MVT 90287
Case 953354
Turn-o-graph
c.1953

US$ 8,000 – 12,000

SOLD US$ 10,625

New York, 5 December, 2018

Automatic stainless-steel
wristwatch and bracelet
Ref. 6202
Turn-o-graph
c.1953

US$ 12,000 – 18,000

SOLD US$ 16,250

ROLEX
OYSTER PERPETUAL
SUPERLATIVE CHRONOMETER
OFFICIALLY CERTIFIED
SWISS

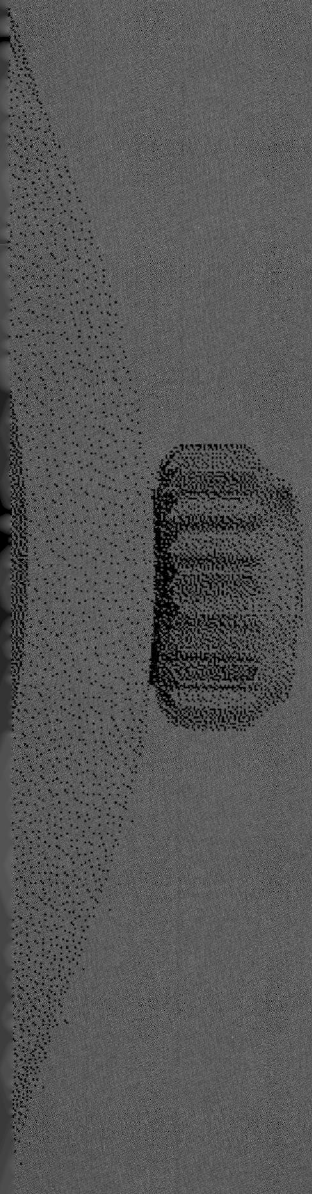

MILGAUSS

Geneva, 16 November, 2004

Rare automatic stainless-steel anti-magnetic wristwatch with centre seconds and bracelet
Ref. 6541
Oyster Perpetual
Milgauss
c.1958

CHF 45,000 – 65,000
US$ 35,700 – 52,000

SOLD CHF 150,000

Reference 6541 Milgauss was launched in 1954. Designed to be used by scientists and those working in areas where exposure to strong magnetic fields was unavoidable, the watch was guaranteed to be anti-magnetic up to 1,000 oersted. Indeed, the word Milgauss means 1,000 gauss. (gauss being a measurement for magnetic induction). Magnetic fields can affect a watch's accuracy at 60 oersted, at 100 oersted the watch ceases to function. The Milgauss overcame the effects of magnetic fields by using anti-magnetic alloys and an iron movement cover.

New York, 16 November, 2004

Rare automatic stainless-steel anti-magnetic wristwatch with bracelet
Ref. 6541
Milgauss
c.1958

US$ 100,000 – 150,000
€ 88,000 – 132,000
HK$ 785,000 – 1,180,000

SOLD US$ 150,000

Geneva, 17 May, 2005

Rare stainless-steel anti-magnetic wristwatch with centre seconds and bracelet
Ref. 6541
Milgauss
c.1955

CHF 45,000 – 65,000
US$ 29,000 – 35,500

SOLD CHF 38,000

Geneva, 15 May, 2011

Rare automatic stainless-steel wristwatch with honeycomb dial and centre seconds
Ref. 6541
Milgauss
*c.*1958

CHF 55,000 – 65,000
US$ 61,000 – 72,000

SOLD CHF 80,500

Geneva, 15 May, 2011

Rare automatic stainless-steel wristwatch with honeycomb dial and centre seconds
Ref. 6541
Milgauss
*c.*1958

CHF 60,000 – 80,000
US$ 66,500 – 88,500

SOLD CHF 74,500

Geneva, 15 May, 2012

Rare automatic stainless-steel
wristwatch with honeycomb
colour-changed dial
and centre seconds
Ref. 6541
Milgauss
c.1956

CHF 60,000 – 80,000
US$ 66,000 – 88,000

SOLD CHF 68,500

London, 8 March, 2016

Very rare automatic stainless-steel
anti-magnetic wristwatch with finely
webbed dial and centre seconds
Ref. 6541
Case 412482
Milgauss
c.1958

£ 25,000 – 35,000
€ 32,000 – 46,000
US$ 35,700 – 50,000

SOLD £ 93,750

Geneva, 16 November, 2004

Automatic stainless-steel
anti-magnetic wristwatch
with centre seconds
Ref. 1019
Oyster Perpetual
Milgauss
*c.*1964

CHF 10,000 – 15,000
US$ 8,000 – 11,000

SOLD CHF 18,000

Like the various tool watches that Rolex has manufactured over the years, Ref. 1019 was introduced in 1956 to meet the demands of the scientific community. Remaining accurate in environments of high magnetic fields, Ref. 1019 has the capability to withstand magnetic fields of up to 1,000 gauss.

Geneva, 16 November, 2004

Automatic stainless-steel
anti-magnetic wristwatch
with centre seconds
and bracelet
Ref. 1019 MVT M209956
Case 1636581
*c.*1968

CHF 15,000 – 25,000
US$ 16,100 – 26,700

SOLD CHF 21,250

Geneva, 16 November, 2008

Automatic stainless-steel anti-magnetic wristwatch with centre seconds and bracelet
Ref. 1019
Oyster Perpetual
Milgauss
c.1967

CHF 20,000 – 30,000
US$ 18,000 – 26,900

SOLD CHF 26,250

Geneva, 16 November, 2008

Automatic stainless-steel anti-magnetic wristwatch with centre seconds
Ref. 1019
Oyster Perpetual
Milgauss
c.1970

CHF 20,000 – 30,000
US$ 18,000 – 26,900

SOLD CHF 24,375

Geneva, 13 November, 2018

Stainless-steel wristwatch
Ref. 1019
Milgauss
c.1967

CHF 15,000 – 25,000
US$ 15,200 – 25,300

SOLD CHF 27,500

ROLEX
OFFICIALLY CERTIFIED
CHRONOMETER
SWISS

GMT-MASTER

New York, 17 October, 2008

Automatic stainless-steel dual-time wristwatch with sweep seconds, bakelite bezel, 24-hour indication and date
Ref. 6542
GMT-Master
c.1957

US$ 40,000 – 50,000

NOT SOLD

The GMT-Master, created in 1954 on the request of Pan American Airlines as well as a European airline, was immediately adopted by pilots, ship's captains, navigators, travellers and members of the Armed Forces, according to a 1960 Rolex catalogue.

Rather than using a steel bezel, as had been introduced on the Submariner, the first GMT Ref. 6542 was launched with a bakelite bezel. Being less reflective than metal, bakelite was favoured by pilots as being less distracting when flying. The colourful bezel also made it very easy to see what time it was 'back home'. The bakelite bezel was soon phased out, however, as it was often found to fracture.

The present watch is accompanied by letters from Rolex addressed to Mr. Ross, Msgt at the US Air Forces, 513th Fighter Interceptor Squadron. The first letter, dated 22 June 1960, describes a crazing of the crystal and a repair by Rolex, mentions the case and reference number and is signed by Mr. Kübel Wilsdorf and another Rolex director at the time. A second letter, as well as an invoice, confirms the repair of the crystal.

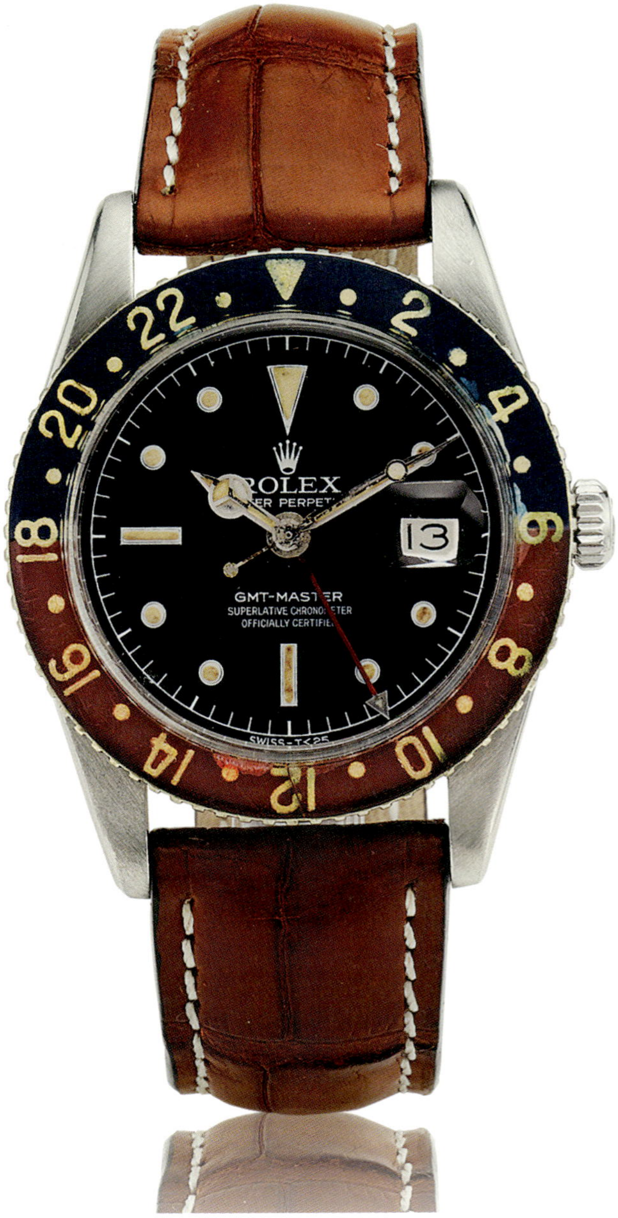

New York, 17 October, 2008

Rare automatic stainless-steel wristwatch with sweep seconds, bakelite bezel, 24-hour indication, date and bracelet
Retailed by Serpico & Laino.
Ref. 6542
GMT-Master
*c.*1955

US$ 100,000 – 150,000

SOLD US$ 107,500

The present watch is especially unusual as the bezel has been well preserved with only minor wear and the dial is signed by the retailer, Serpico y Laino of Caracas, Venezuela, one of the most important retailers in the Americas. In addition to this, the outside of the case back is marked 'S y L Acero' ('S and L Steel'). Over the years, most retailers' marks on the case backs are lost due to wear and polish. The rich brown tropical colour to the dial also enhances the watch's overal aesthetic charm.

Geneva, 16 November, 2008

Rare automatic stainless-steel
wristwatch with centre seconds, date,
24-hour indication on a bakelite bezel
and stainless-steel bracelet
Ref. 6542
Oyster
GMT-Master
*c.*1959

CHF 50,000 – 70,000
US$ 44,800 – 63,000

SOLD CHF 56,250

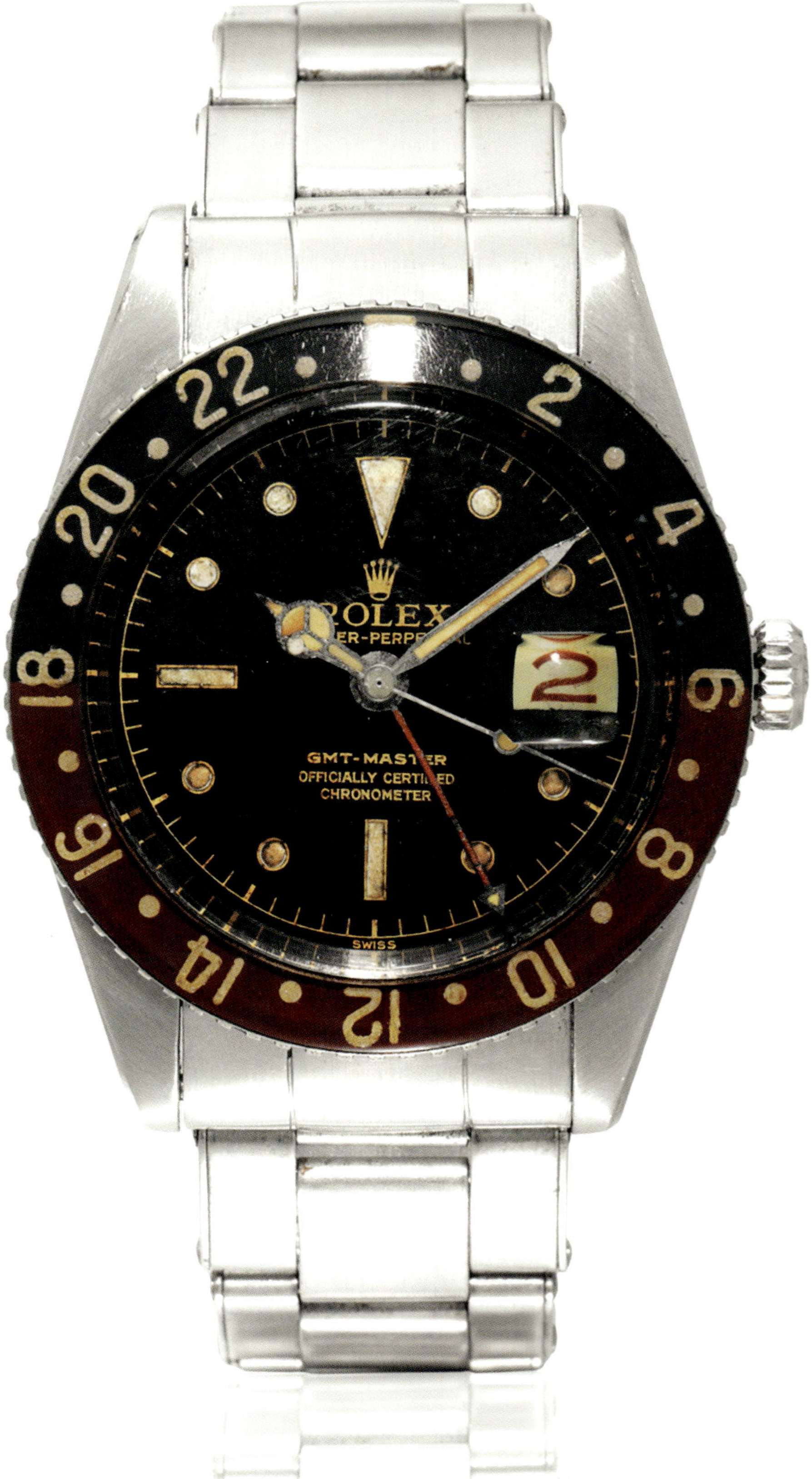

New York, 6 December, 2011

Rare automatic stainless-steel wristwatch with sweep seconds, bakelite bezel, 24-hour indication and date
Ref. 6542
Case 356110
GMT-Master
c.1959

US$ 30,000 – 40,000
HK$ 234,000 – 312,000

NOT SOLD

Geneva, 11 May, 2013

Automatic stainless-steel wristwatch with centre seconds, bakelite bezel, 24-hour indication, date and bracelet
Ref. 6542
Case 482123
GMT-Master 'Pan Am'
c.1959

CHF 24,000 – 34,000
US$ 25,500 – 36,100

SOLD CHF 30,000

New York, 10 December, 2013

Extremely rare automatic yellow-gold dual-time wristwatch with date, centre seconds, bakelite bezel and bracelet
Ref. 6542
Case 424243
GMT-Master
*c.*1958

US$ 80,000 – 120,000
€ 59,500 – 89,000
HK$ 625,000 – 935,000

SOLD US$ 125,000

New York, 10 December, 2014

Rare stainless-steel dual-time wristwatch with date and bakelite bezel
Ref. 6542
Case 212425
GMT-Master
*c.*1956

US$ 50,000 – 70,000
€ 39,800 – 56,000
HK$ 388,000 – 545,000

SOLD US$ 62,500

New York, 17 October, 2008

Automatic yellow-gold dual-time wristwatch with sweep seconds, date, 24-hour indication and bracelet
Ref 1675
GMT-Master
c.1967

US$ 25,000 – 35,000

NOT SOLD

Introduced in 1959 and only discontinued in 1980, Ref. 1675 – the successor to the 6542 – is one of the longest produced watches in Rolex's history.

1 New York, 17 October, 2008

Automatic yellow-gold dual-time wristwatch with sweep seconds, date, 24-hour indication and bracelet
Ref. 1675
GMT-Master
c.1977

US$ 18,000 – 22,000

NOT SOLD

1

2 New York, 17 October, 2008

Automatic 18k yellow-gold dual-time wristwatch with sweep seconds, date, 24-hour indication and bracelet
Ref. 1675
GMT-Master
c.1963

US$ 15,000 – 20,000

NOT SOLD

2

3 Geneva, 12 November, 2013

Rare automatic yellow-gold dual-time wristwatch with centre seconds, date and bracelet
Ref. 1675
Case 1360460
GMT-Master ‘no crown guards’
c.1966

CHF 20,000 – 30,000
US$ 21,600 – 32,400

SOLD CHF 32,500

3

Geneva, 13 May, 2015

Rare automatic yellow-gold dual-time wristwatch with centre seconds, date and bracelet
Ref. 1675
Case 3315514
GMT-Master
c.1972

CHF 15,000 – 20,000
US$ 15,400 – 20,500

SOLD CHF 18,750

1 Geneva, 13 November, 2018

Stainless-steel dual-time wristwatch with date, pointed crown guards, black gloss dial and bracelet; original accessories
Ref. 1675
GMT-Master
c.1964

CHF 15,000 – 25,000
US$ 15,200 – 25,300

SOLD CHF 46,250

1

2 Geneva, 13 November, 2018

Rare yellow-gold wristwatch with 24-hour hand, date, no crown guards and original Rolex guarantee
Ref. 1675
GMT-Master
c.1966

CHF 20,000 – 30,000
US$ 20,200 – 30,300

SOLD CHF 40,000

2

Geneva, 13 November, 2018

Yellow-gold dual-time wristwatch with underline dial and no crown guards
Ref. 1675
GMT-Master
c.1963

CHF 30,000 – 50,000
US$ 30,300 – 50,500

SOLD CHF 57,500

This watch is an example of the early iterations of Ref. 1675, the direct successor to the 6542, which were produced without crown guards; these would be added in later models. Other vintage elements to this watch are the extremely attractive leaf-style hands and nipple indexes, both of which have aged, taking on a beautiful brown patina.

Not only does this watch represent the transition between the old and the new GMT models but also the emerging use of tritium rather than radium. As such, the dial is marked with an underline below the SCOC text above the 6 index.

1 Geneva, 12 November, 2019

Yellow-gold dual-time wristwatch
with date and bracelet
Ref. 1675 MVT D'062'793
Case 1'741'333
GMT-Master 'Concorde'
c.1967

CHF 30,000 – 50,000
US$ 30,200 – 50,500

SOLD CHF 32,500

1

2 New York, 11 December, 2019

Automatic stainless-steel dual-time
wristwatch with date and bracelet
Ref. 1675 MVT D941623
Case 3163341
GMT-Master
c.1972

US$ 12,000 – 18,000
€ 10,800 – 16,200
HK$ 94,500 – 142,000

SOLD US$ 27,500

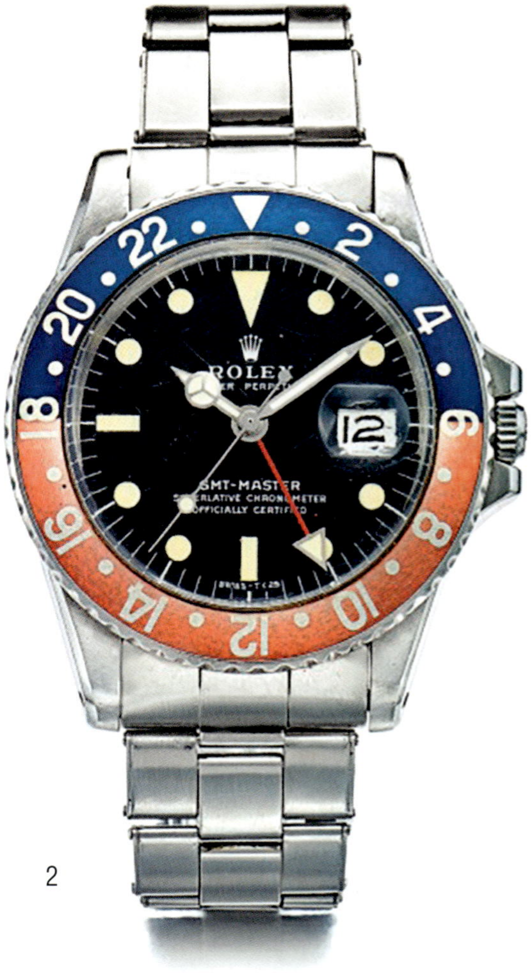

2

Geneva, 13 November, 2018

Yellow-gold dual-time
wristwatch with date
and bracelet
Ref. 16758
GMT-Master
*c.*1984

CHF 18,000 – 30,000
US$ 18,200 – 30,300

SOLD CHF 27,500

To sit alongside the robust stainless-steel version of its famed pilot's watch, Rolex also made luxurious 18k yellow-gold variations of the GMT-Master. The yellow-gold GMT-Master 16758 was first introduced in 1981, and only remained in production for a relatively short time until it was discontinued in 1988. The use of the 24-hour marked bezel in conjunction with the 24-hour hand allows users to simultaneously reference a second time zone. Although the steel counterpart of the 16758 was fitted with an acrylic crystal, Rolex opted for modern scratch-resistant sapphire for the crystal of the yellow-gold version.

1 New York, 4 June, 2019

Automatic yellow-gold dual-time wristwatch with centre seconds, date and bracelet
Ref. 16758
GMT-Master
c.1984

US$ 8,000 – 12,000

SOLD US$ 21,250

1

2 New York, 20 August, 2019

Yellow-gold wristwatch with bracelet
Ref. 16758
GMT-Master
c.1981

US$ 15,000 – 25,000

SOLD US$ 23,750

3 Hong Kong, 9 October, 2020

Diamond- and ruby-set yellow-gold dual-time wristwatch with date and bracelet
Ref. 16758
GMT-Master
c.1987

HK$ 180,000 – 240,000

SOLD HK$ 226,800

2

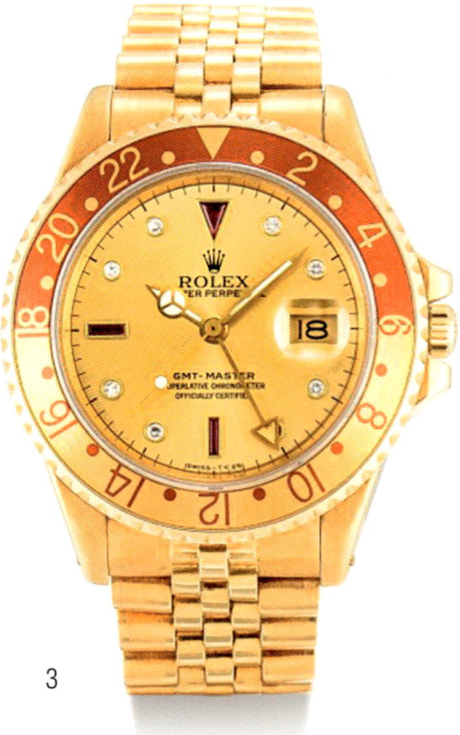

3

Hong Kong, 26 May, 2014

Automatic diamond- and black sapphire-set yellow-gold dual-time wristwatch with centre seconds, date and bracelet
Ref. 116758 SANR
Case M581992
GMT-Master II
*c.*2007

HK$ 300,000 – 450,000
US$ 38,700 – 58,500

SOLD HK$ 350,000

This impressive and rare timepiece is in direct lineage to the legendary 16758 'SARU' which was, in the mid-eighties, not only one of the first factory-set Rolexes in history but also the first GMT set with precious stones. The bezel is enhanced with 36 diamonds and 12 black sapphires, furthermore, the case is set with 76 diamonds.

Hong Kong, 2 October, 2017

Rare automatic diamond- and sapphire-set white-gold dual-time wristwatch with date and bracelet
Ref. 116759
Case V505710
GMT-Master II
*c.*2008

HK$ 480,000 – 650,000
US$ 61,500 – 83,500

SOLD HK$ 625,000

Rolex first launched these exceptional white-gold and gemstone-set versions of the iconic GMT-Master II in 2007. Three extravagant versions of this reference can be found: the 116759 SANR with diamonds and black sapphires; the 116759 SARU with diamonds, sapphires and rubies; and the 116759 SA with diamonds and blue sapphires.

Geneva, 14 May, 2014

Rare automatic diamond-set
white-gold dual-time wristwatch
with date and bracelet; bezel set
with diamonds, sapphires and rubies
Ref. 116759
Case M991601
GMT-Master II SARU
c.2010

CHF 30,000 – 50,000
US$ 34,100 – 57,000

SOLD CHF 52,500

GMT-MASTER II Ref. 116749 SABLNR

Hong Kong, 2 October, 2018

Rare diamond- and sapphire-set white-gold dual-time wristwatch with date and bracelet
Ref. 116749 SABLNR
Case 3961v664
GMT-Master II
*c.*2017

HK$ 600,000 – 800,000
US$ 76,500 – 102,000

SOLD HK$ 937,500

Reference 116710 has immediately earned its title as the fans' favourite GMT-Master II after its debut at the 2013 Baselworld. With the strong blue-and-black colour contrast cerachrom bezel, this watch became known as the 'Batman'.

The reference 116749 SABLNR GMT-Master II – introduced in 2017 – houses the same case and movement as Ref. 11670 but, instead of being made of cerachrom, the bezel is set with blue sapphires, black sapphires and diamonds.

ROLEX
GMT-MASTER II
SUPERLATIVE CHRONOMETER
OFFICIALLY CERTIFIED
SWISS MADE

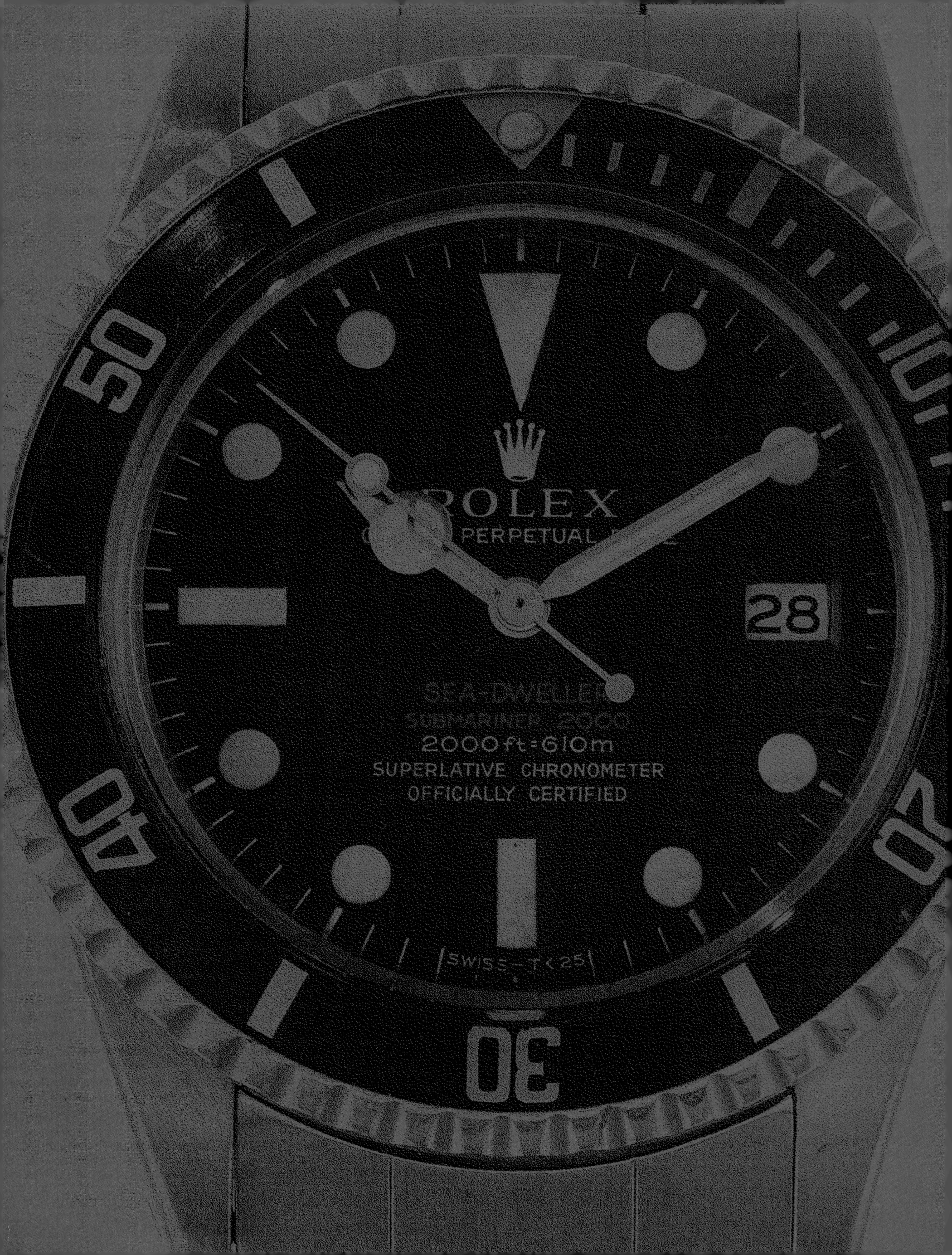

ROLEX
PERPETUAL
28
SEA-DWELLER
SUBMARINER 2000
2000ft=610m
SUPERLATIVE CHRONOMETER
OFFICIALLY CERTIFIED

SEA-DWELLER

Geneva, 15 May, 2007

Rare automatic stainless-steel wristwatch with centre seconds, date and bracelet
Ref 1665
Sea-Dweller
c.1971

CHF 15,000 – 20,000
US$ 12,500 – 16,600

SOLD CHF 38,400

Rolex developed the Sea-Dweller model in close connection with the French deep-sea diving firm Comex (Compagnie Maritime d'Expertises). When divers would go under water and come back to the surface, their watches would tend to fill with helium and would then be vulnerable to damage or explosion from an imbalance in pressure.

To counteract this, Rolex developed the gas escape valve at 9 o'clock that the user could depress to release the helium from the case.

The first generation of the reference 1665 Sea-Dweller was produced in 1967. At the time, the case back was engraved with words 'patent pending' since Rolex was still waiting for the helium valve escapement patent, testing this new technology on Submariner references 5513 and 5514. It was tested and approved for depths down to 2,000 feet, or roughly 610 metres.

The first generation of Ref. 1665 featured 'Sea-Dweller Submariner 2000' in red printing. As these dials were in production for a limited period of time, they are much more collectible in the market today. Collectors have identified four main evolutions up to 1977, the year Rolex introduced 'Great White' dials.

New York, 23 April, 2008

Automatic stainless-steel
wristwatch with sweep seconds,
date and bracelet
Ref. 1665
Oyster Perpetual
Sea-Dweller patent pending
c.1967

US$ 65,000 – 85,000

SOLD US$ 93,400

New York, 17 October, 2008

Automatic stainless-steel wristwatch
with sweep seconds,
date and bracelet
Ref. 1665 'Double Red'
Sea-Dweller
c.1972

US$ 25,000 – 35,000

SOLD US$ 33,750

Geneva, 13 November, 2011

Rare automatic stainless-steel
wristwatch with centre seconds, date,
bracelet and Rolex patent back
Made for Comex
Ref. 1665
Sea-Dweller
c.1981

CHF 50,000 – 70,000
US$ 55,500 – 78,000

SOLD CHF 62,500

1 Geneva, 15 May, 2012

Stainless-steel wristwatch
with centre seconds, date
and bracelet
Ref. 1665 Mark I 'Double Red'
Sea-Dweller patent pending
c.1967

CHF 30,000 – 50,000
US$ 33,000 – 55,000

SOLD CHF 35,000

2 Geneva, 15 May, 2012

Stainless-steel wristwatch with
centre seconds, date and bracelet
Ref. 1665 Mark I 'Double Red'
Sea-Dweller patent pending
c.1967

CHF 60,000 – 90,000
US$ 66,500 – 100,000

SOLD CHF 72,100

This model was put into production before the official patent for the new helium valve had been granted, hence the inscription 'patent pending' on the case back, which makes it much sought after by collectors.

According to most Rolex scholars, only 150 pieces were produced from this period, with serial numbers ranging from 1.7 and 2.2 million.

1

2

New York, 10 June, 2013

Extremely rare automatic stainless-steel diver's wristwatch with date, centre seconds and bracelet; no gas-escape valve
Ref. 1665 'Single Red'
Case 1602928
Sea-Dweller
*c.*1967

US$ 60,000 – 80,000
€ 46,100 – 61,500

SOLD US$ 383,000

This watch is a fascinating and little-known prototype model that marked the transition between designs, a watch made in small numbers only available to professional divers for field testing. Prior to the availability of Ref. 1665 to the general public, these test models had a thinner case profile, and did not feature the gas escape valve. In their experimental usage, many of these watches did not survive the pressures of deep-sea diving.

These prototype watches feature dials markedly different to the standard 1665 dial. Referred to today as the Mark 00, or 'Single Red' Sea-Dweller dial, the first line, 'Sea-Dweller', is printed in red, and the next line, 'Submariner 500 M – 1650 FT', is printed in white. (Later examples read 'Submariner 2000', and both lines are red, hence the phrase 'Double Red' Sea-Dweller.) In the line below the Rolex logo, the word 'Date' is printed in a larger font than the preceding words 'Oyster Perpetual'. It is thought that of the few such dials created, many were replaced during services by Rolex, making the present watch all the more remarkable, as it was serviced by Rolex in 1993.

The present model, then, stands apart from even the most often aspired-to 'dream' watch of the Rolex sports model collector, the comparatively commonplace 'Double Red' Sea-Dweller. The 'Single Red' Sea-Dweller is mentioned only in scholarly texts, and the highly infrequent appearance of such watches at auction creates a frenzy among collectors. This watch was with the same owner, an accomplished American diver, for nearly 45 years, since its creation in the late 1960s.

Geneva, 14 May, 2014

Automatic stainless-steel wristwatch with centre seconds, date and bracelet
Ref. 1665 'Double-red'
Case 4135227
Sea-Dweller
c.1978

CHF 15,000 – 20,000
US$ 17,100 – 22,800

SOLD CHF 23,750

Geneva, 13 May, 2015

Rare automatic stainless-steel wristwatch with centre seconds, date, bracelet and Rolex patent back
Made for Comex
Ref. 1665
Case 6221315
Sea-Dweller 2170
c.1980

CHF 40,000 – 60,000
US$ 40,900 – 61,500

SOLD CHF 65,000

1 Geneva, 14 May, 2016

Automatic stainless-steel diver's wristwatch with centre seconds, date and bracelet
Ref. 1665 'Double Red'
Case 3567014
Sea-Dweller 2000ft=610m
*c.*1972

CHF 10,000 – 15,000
US$ 10,300 – 15,500

SOLD CHF 17,500

2 Geneva, 13 November, 2018

Stainless-steel wristwatch with date and bracelet
Ref. 1665 'Double Red'
Sea-Dweller
*c.*1978

CHF 30,000 – 50,000
US$ 30,300 – 50,500

SOLD CHF 52,500

1

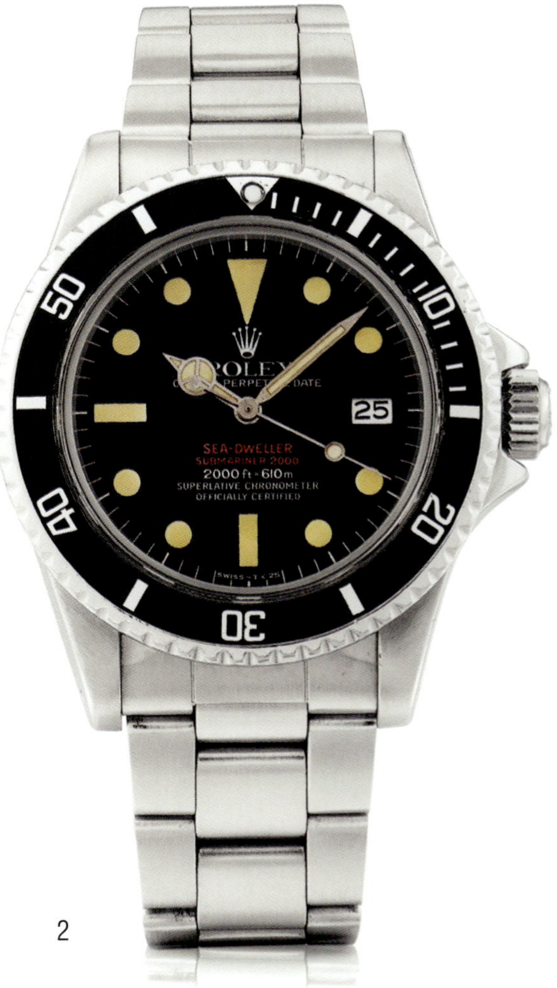

2

Geneva, 12 November, 2019

Stainless-steel wristwatch with date,
helium escape valve and bracelet
Ref. 1665 MVT D'991'828
Case 1'760'323
Sea-Dweller 'Double Red'
*c.*1968

CHF 35,000 – 55,000
US$ 35,300 – 55,500

NOT SOLD

Geneva, 12 May, 2019

Stainless-steel wristwatch
with date and bracelet
Property of Comex diver
Thèo Mavrostomos
Ref. 16600
Sea-Dweller 'Comex'
c.1998

CHF 80,000 – 120,000
US$ 80,000 – 120,000

SOLD CHF 93,750

Ref. 16600 – the longest lasting Sea-Dweller reference – was available from 1989 to 2009. During its long production, the luminous material evolved from tritium to Luminova and, finally, Super Luminova.

The emergence and subsequent progression of scuba diving in industry during the 1960s and '70s called for very specially designed equipment. Watches in particular played a significant role in the work of professional divers and were tools relied upon heavily. This new demand for precision timepieces that could tolerate the stresses of prolonged deep-water submersion sparked a period of significant innovation within the major Swiss watch manufacturers, keen to capitalise on a fresh and growing market.

Helium atoms represent the smallest naturally occurring particles of any gas and, as such, could breach the seals and seep into watch cases. The pressure difference caused by this was identified as the leading cause of breaks while decompressing after a dive. The Helium Escape Valve (HEV) was primarily introduced in the '60s and first appeared on Submariners before they were then adopted and solely used on the Sea-Dweller.

This example was issued in 1998 to respected deep-sea diver Thèo Mavrostomos, who went on to become a Rolex brand ambassador, appearing in adverts for the Sea-Dweller. Mavrostomos, who worked with COMEX for 20 years, was Awarded the French Order of Merit in 1997 for achieving a simulated 'saturation' dive of 701m during COMEX's Hydra X trials. The case back has been inscribed to celebrate this tremendous event and the watch still retains all its original accessories.

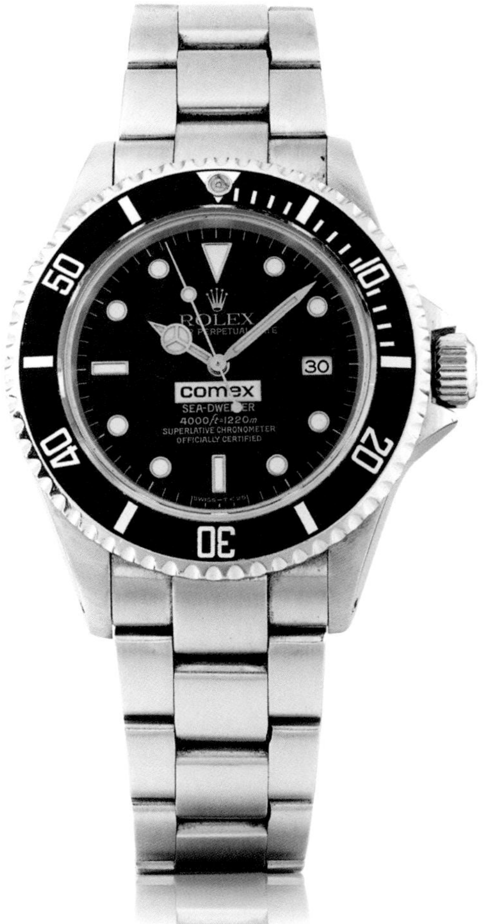

Geneva, 13 November, 2018

Stainless-steel wristwatch with
date and bracelet
Ref. 16660
Sea-Dweller 'Comex'
c.1984

CHF 30,000 – 50,000
US$ 30,300 – 50,500

SOLD CHF 67,500

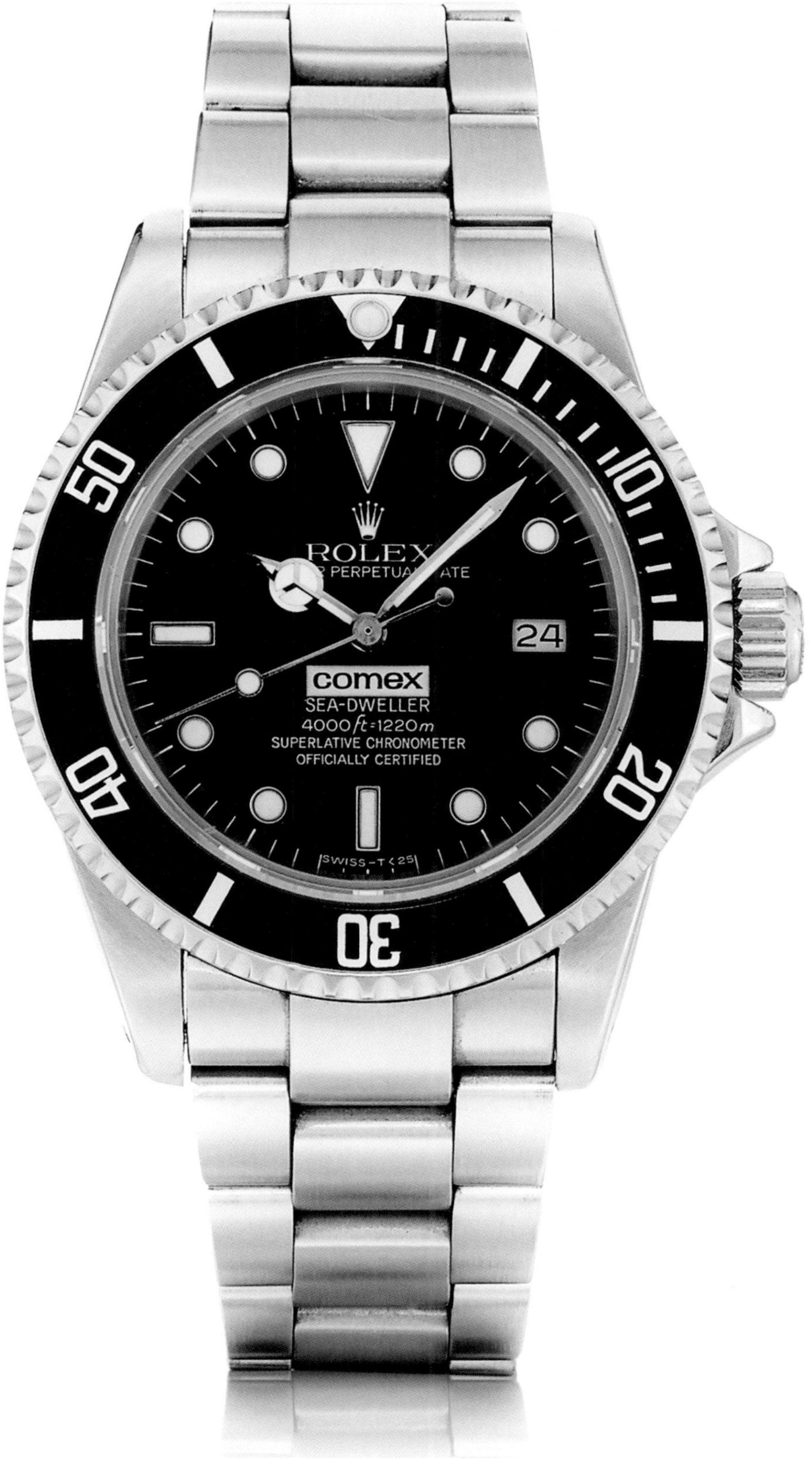

24
2
22
20
18
16
14
12
10
ROLEX
OYSTER PERPETUAL DATE
PLORER II
8
SWISS – T < 25

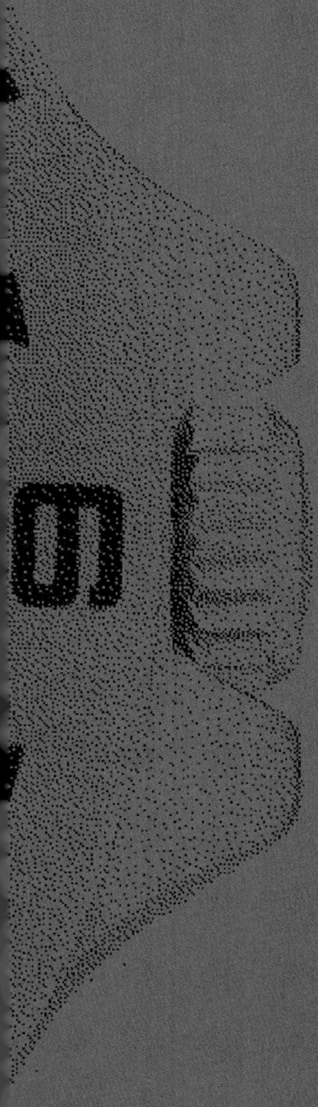

EXPLORER

1 London, 19 March, 2003

Automatic stainless-steel wristwatch with centre seconds and bracelet
Ref. 1016
Oyster Perpetual Explorer
*c.*1974

£ 1,600 – 1,900
€ 2,450 – 2,900

SOLD £ 2,400

2 London, 19 March, 2003

Automatic stainless-steel wristwatch with centre seconds and bracelet
Ref. 1016
Oyster Perpetual Explorer
*c.*1967

£ 1,500 – 2,000
€ 2,300 – 3,050

SOLD £ 1,920

Since its introduction in 1953 and the first summit ascent of the Everest in the same year, the Rolex Explorer has embodied the pioneering and adventurous spirit of the brand.

The Explorer I Ref. 1016 was produced by Rolex for nearly 30 years, from the early 1960s until about 1989. During this period, the model was updated but never completely changed. Its classic look and robust design have made it an enduring model, appealing as much to the sportsman and adventurer as to the watch connoisseur.

1

2

1 London, 19 March, 2003

Automatic stainless-steel wristwatch
with centre seconds and bracelet
Ref. 1016
Oyster Perpetual Explorer
c.1960

£ 1,500 – 2,000
€ 2,300 – 3,050

SOLD £ 1,920

2 London, 19 March, 2003

Automatic stainless-steel wristwatch
with centre seconds and bracelet
Ref. 1016
Oyster Perpetual Explorer
c.1987

£ 1,600 – 1,900
€ 2,400 – 2,900

SOLD £ 2,400

1

2

1 Geneva, 16 November, 2004

Automatic stainless-steel
wristwatch with centre seconds
and bracelet
Ref. 1016
Oyster Perpetual Explorer
c.1966

CHF 3,500 – 4,500
US$ 2,800 – 3,600

SOLD CHF 4,200

1

2 Geneva, 16 November, 2004

Automatic stainless-steel
wristwatch with centre seconds
and bracelet
Ref. 1016
Oyster Perpetual Explorer
c.1975

CHF 2,800 – 3,500
US$ 2,250 – 2,800

SOLD CHF 4,800

2

Geneva, 11 May, 2013

Automatic stainless-steel wristwatch with centre seconds, bracelet and complete correspondence
Supplied for the SANAE 27 Antartic expedition
Ref. 1016
Case 5711286
Explorer
*c.*1986

CHF 30,000 – 40,000
US$ 31,800 – 42,400

SOLD CHF 37,500

The present watch belonged to Graham Blyth a member of the SANAE (South African National Antarctic Expedition) 27 expedition. The purpose of the mission was for scientific, meteorological and photographical research of the land and nature of the Antarctic.

The SANAE team endured exceptionally harsh conditions: prolonged Antarctic nights, temperatures as low as -50 °C, strong magnetic fields, wind and storms. Blyth was sponsored by Rolex and they supplied one of their most robust models, an Explorer I Ref. 1016, for the expedition.

1 Geneva, 13 November, 2018

Stainless-steel wristwatch
with 24-hour indication,
date and bracelet
Ref. 1655
Oyster Perpetual Date
Explorer II
c.1982

CHF 12,000 – 18,000

SOLD CHF 21,250

2 New York, 4 June, 2019

Automatic stainless-steel
dual-time wristwatch
with date and bracelet
Ref. 1655
Oyster Perpetual Date
Explorer II
'Steve McQueen'
c.1971

US$ 25,000 – 35,000

SOLD US$ 31,250

Originally developed in 1971 for cave explorers, the Explorer II Ref. 1655 is the first reference in this family of Rolex watches. The Explorer 1655 is often referred to by the nickname 'Freccione' (Italian for 'arrow') thanks to its prominent orange arrow-tipped 24-hour hand. By pointing to the fixed 24-hour marked bezel, the 24-hour hand serves as a prominent AM/PM indicator; practical for those who spend extended periods exploring in hazardous conditions and might otherwise become disorientated.

1

2

1 New York, 20 August, 2019

Stainless-steel wristwatch
with bracelet
Ref. 1655
Explorer II
*c.*1984

US$ 15,000 – 25,000

SOLD US$ 21,250

1

2 New York, 19 September, 2019

Automatic stainless-steel
dual-time wristwatch with date
and bracelet
Ref. 1655
Explorer II
*c.*1983

US$ 6,000 – 8,000

SOLD US$ 11,875

2

1 New York, 1 December, 2019

Automatic stainless-steel
wristwatch with 24-hour
indication, date and bracelet
Ref. 1655
Explorer II
c.1975

US$ 20,000 – 30,000

NOT SOLD

1

2 London, 5 December, 2019

Stainless-steel dual-time
wristwatch with date and bracelet
Ref. 1655
Oyster Perpetual Date
Explorer II
'Steve McQueen'
c.1984

£ 9,000 – 12,000

SOLD £ 15,000

2

1 Hong Kong, 8 April, 2020

Stainless-steel wristwatch
with 24-hour indication,
date and bracelet
Ref. 1655
Explorer II
c.1984

HK$ 160,000 – 200,000

NOT SOLD

2 New York, 4 September, 2020

Automatic stainless-steel
wristwatch with 24-hour
indication, date and bracelet
Ref. 1655
Oyster Perpetual Date
Explorer II
c.1971

US$ 8,000 – 12,000

SOLD US$ 22,680

1

2

Geneva, 12 November, 2013

Stainless-steel, dual-time wristwatch with centre seconds, date and bracelet
Ref. 16550
Case 8399404
Explorer II
'Rolex Gold Cup Champion'
*c.*1984

CHF 10,000 – 15,000
US$ 10,800 – 16,200

SOLD CHF 11,250

Ref. 16550 was first launched by Rolex in the mid '80s and produced for only about 5 years. Designed with a 24-hour bezel and a luminous 24-hour large arrow hand, this is a watch that was designed for those who spend long periods of time in dark environments, such as cavers.

1 Geneva, 13 November, 2018

Automatic stainless-steel dual-time wristwatch with centre seconds, date, 24-hour indication and bracelet
Ref. 16550
Case 906995
Explorer II S.C. 'Rail dial'
*c.*1986

CHF 8,000 – 10,000
US$ 8,400 – 10,400

SOLD CHF 15,000

2 Geneva, 13 November, 2018

Stainless-steel wristwatch with 24-hour indication, date and bracelet
Ref. 16550
Explorer II
*c.*1984

CHF 6,000 – 8,000

SOLD CHF 7,500

1

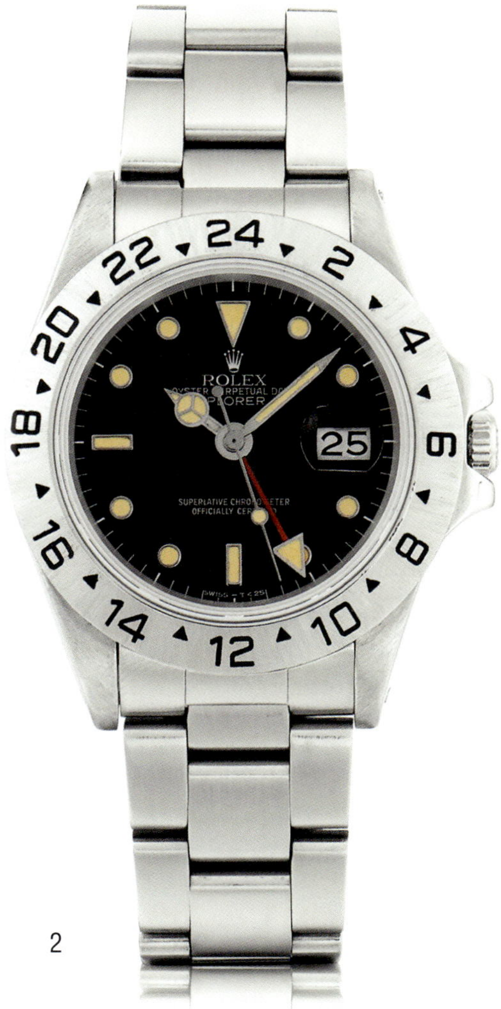

2

1 Dubai, 24 March, 2019

Stainless-steel dual-time wristwatch
with date, 24-hour indication and
bracelet
Made for President Hafez Al-Assad
Ref. 16550
Explorer II
c.1988

US$ 15,000 – 20,000

SOLD US$ 33,750

1

2 New York, 4 September, 2020

Automatic stainless-steel wristwatch
with 24-hour indication, date,
and bracelet
Ref. 16550
Explorer II
c.1971

US$ 8,000 – 12,000

SOLD US$ 22,680

2

London, 22 September, 2015

Rare automatic stainless-steel dual-time wristwatch with centre seconds, date, 24-hour indication and bracelet
Made for the 22nd Special Air Service Regiment – SAS 'Who dares wins'
Ref. 216570
Case G733319
Explorer II
*c.*2012

£ 10,000 – 15,000
€ 14,300 – 21,400
US$ 15,600 – 23,400

SOLD £ 17,500

The British Special Air Service (SAS) was founded in 1941 as a Special Operations division of the British Army and has ever since remained one of the most respected military organisations in the world. The unit is thought to employ 500 active soldiers who have undergone extreme recruitment and training programmes. Perpetuating their long-lasting relationship with military forces, in 2012, Rolex granted the SAS soldiers the opportunity to acquire a highly personal and exclusive example of the Explorer II, Ref. 216570.

Zurich, 25 June, 2019

Stainless-steel dual-time wristwatch
with date and bracelet
Ref. 216570
Explorer II
*c.*2012

CHF 3,000 – 5,000

SOLD CHF 6,000

1 London, 17 July, 2019

Military stainless-steel dual-time wristwatch with date and bracelet
Made for the 22nd Special Air Service Regiment
Ref. 216570
Explorer II
c.2012

£ 12,000 – 18,000

SOLD £ 25,000

1

2 London, 2 October, 2020

Stainless-steel dual-time wristwatch with date and bracelet
Ref. 216570
Explorer II
c.2019

£ 4,000 – 6,000

SOLD £ 6,930

2

ROLEX
OYSTER PERPETUAL
TRU-BEAT
SUPERLATIVE CHRONOMETER
OFFICIALLY CERTIFIED
SWISS

TRU-BEAT

Geneva, 19 November, 2003

Rare and unusual automatic stainless-steel wristwatch with jumping-centre seconds and bracelet
Ref. 6556
Oyster Perpetual Tru-beat
c.1956

CHF 15,000 – 20,000
US$ 12,000 – 16,000

SOLD CHF 18,000

The origins of this reference lie in the creation, by the movement maker Chezard, of the calibre 115, a dead-seconds movement.

Following this, companies such as Omega and Doxa created their own versions. Rolex, unusually, also followed the lead by modifying their calibre 1030 to produce the 1040. As a movement, it is extremely difficult to work on, a fact borne out by the many Tru-beat watches that have had the dead-seconds mechanism stripped out. This also means that there are very few intact examples of the Tru-beat.

New York, 17 October, 2008

Automatic stainless-steel wristwatch with dead-beat centre seconds and bracelet
Ref. 6556
Tru-beat
*c.*1956

US$ 14,500 – 16,500

NOT SOLD

Rolex launched this model, Ref. 6556, in the mid 1950s. It features dead-beat centre seconds, one of the most unusual complications that Rolex produced. Whereas the seconds hand on a standard lever escapement will sweep around the dial, the hand on a dead-beat escapement will stop slightly at each second and then jump to the next, similar to the manner in which the seconds hand on a detent chronometer would function.

The Tru-beat was designed to have a seconds hand that jumped exactly to each seconds marker rather than moving several times each second, as is more normally found in mechanical watches. To emphasise the point, the original Rolex advertisements for the Tru-beat showed an image of a grasshopper jumping to each calibrated second on the watch's dial.

Geneva, 16 November, 2008

Rare and unusual automatic stainless-steel wristwatch with jumping-centre seconds and bracelet
Ref. 6556
Oyster Perpetual Tru-beat
*c.*1956

CHF 12,000 – 18,000
US$ 10,800 – 16,200

SOLD CHF 13,750

1 New York, 20 October, 2009

Rare automatic stainless-steel
wristwatch with dead-beat
centre seconds
Ref. 6556
Tru-beat
c.1959

US$ 7,500 – 10,000

NOT SOLD

1

2 Hong Kong, 6 October, 2015

Rare and unusual automatic
stainless-steel wristwatch
with jumping-centre seconds
and bracelet
Ref. 6556
Case 139035
Oyster Perpetual Tru-beat
c.1956

HK$ 50,000 – 70,000

SOLD HK$ 93,750

2

SATURDAY
ROLEX
OYSTER PERPETUAL
DAY-DATE
18
SUPERLATIVE CHRONOMETER
OFFICIALLY CERTIFIED
SWISS MADE

DAY-DATE

New York, 5 December, 2005

Automatic white-gold wristwatch with sweep seconds, calendar and bracelet
Ref. 1803
Oyster Perpetual Day-Date
*c.*1965

US$ 5,500 – 6,500

SOLD US$ 9,600

Ref. 1803 appeared in the 1961 Rolex catalogues, together with references 1804 and 1806.

Geneva, 13 November, 2018

White-gold wristwatch with day, date and bracelet made for the Sultanate of Oman
Ref. 1803
Khanjar Day-Date
*c.*1975

CHF 28,000 – 35,000
US$ 28,300 – 35,300

SOLD CHF 35,000

Geneva, 12 May, 2019

Yellow-gold wristwatch with day, date, bracelet and rare linear geometric engraved dial
Ref. 1803
Day-Date
c.1963

CHF 45,000 – 70,000
US$ 45,000 – 70,000

SOLD CHF 56,250

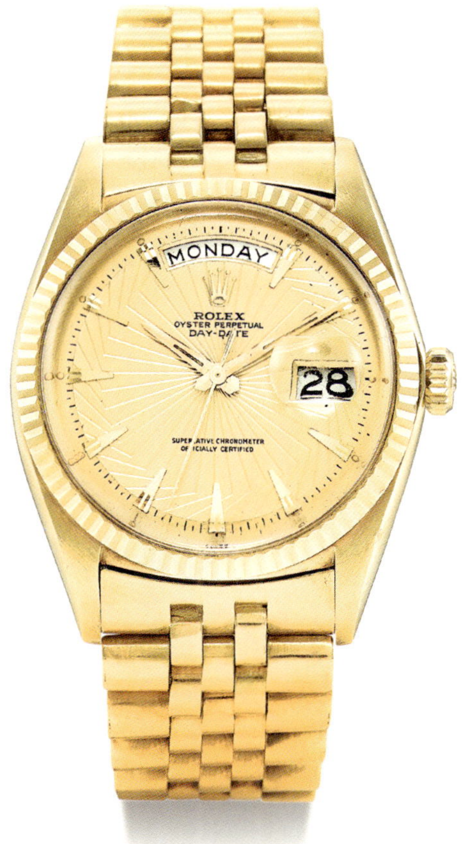

Geneva, 12 November, 2019

Yellow-gold wristwatch with day, date, bracelet and red Stella dial
Ref. 1803 MVT DD'974'564
Case 4'211'888
Day-Date 'Stella'
c.1975

CHF 30,000 – 40,000
US$ 30,200 – 40,300

SOLD CHF 43,750

Geneva, 12 November, 2019

White-gold wristwatch with day, date, bracelet and blue Stella dial
Ref. 1803 MVT DD'656'045
Case 3'634'352
Day-Date 'Stella'
c.1974

CHF 20,000 – 30,000
US$ 20,200 – 30,200

SOLD CHF 58,750

Geneva, 12 November, 2019

White-gold wristwatch with day, date, bracelet and green Stella dial
Ref. 1803 MVT DD'700'429
Case 3'634'416
Day-Date 'Stella'
c.1974

CHF 30,000 – 50,000
US$ 30,200 – 50,500

SOLD CHF 55,000

1 Geneva, 14 May, 2014

Very rare automatic diamond-set platinum wristwatch with centre seconds, day, date, Stella dial and bracelet
Ref. 1804
Case 4223670
Day-Date
c.1976

CHF 70,000 – 80,000
US$ 79,500 – 91,000

SOLD CHF 68,750

2 Geneva, 14 May, 2016

Rare automatic diamond-set platinum wristwatch with centre seconds, day, date and bracelet
Ref 1804
Case 1999039
Day-Date
c.1968

CHF 45,000 – 65,000
US$ 46,300 – 67,000

SOLD CHF 50,000

1

2

2 The Rolex Day-Date reference 1804, produced since the early 1960s, is characterised by the precious bezel set with diamonds. The dial, available in a large number of variants, has a flared edge and is called a pie-pan.

The movement is cal. 1555, replaced by 1556 c.1965. It is available combined with the typical President bracelet but also with leather strap and matching buckle.

Geneva, 13 May, 2018

Very rare automatic diamond-set platinum wristwatch with centre seconds, day, date and laquered Stella dial
Ref 1804
Case 2685097
Day-Date
c.1971

CHF 50,000 – 80,000
US$ 46,300 – 67,000

NOT SOLD

This example of a Ref. 1804, featuring a burgundy Stella dial and a combination of diamonds on the dial as well as on the bezel, is one of the rarest examples to have recently appeared at auction.

Geneva, 12 May, 2019

Platinum, white-gold and diamond-set wristwatch with day, date and bracelet
Ref. 1804
Day-Date Octopussy
c.1971

CHF 100,000 – 200,000
US$ 100,000 – 200,000

SOLD CHF 125,000

This wristwatch is a rare example in platinum with diamond-set indexes, a gorgeous oxblood enamel lacquered dial and a white-gold bracelet. Rolex only produced these dials from the 1960s to the 1990s. The bezel is adorned with 46 brilliant-cut diamonds. The Rolex white-gold President bracelet is decorated with two rows of brilliant-cut diamonds and a central row of baguette-cut diamonds..

Geneva, 12 May, 2019

Diamond-set yellow-gold wristwatch
with day, date and bracelet
Made for The Sultanate of Oman
Ref. 1804 MVT DD'172'590
Case 4'198'781
Day-Date 'Octopussy Khanjar'
c.1976

CHF 60,000 – 100,000
US$ 60,500 – 101,000

SOLD CHF 100,000

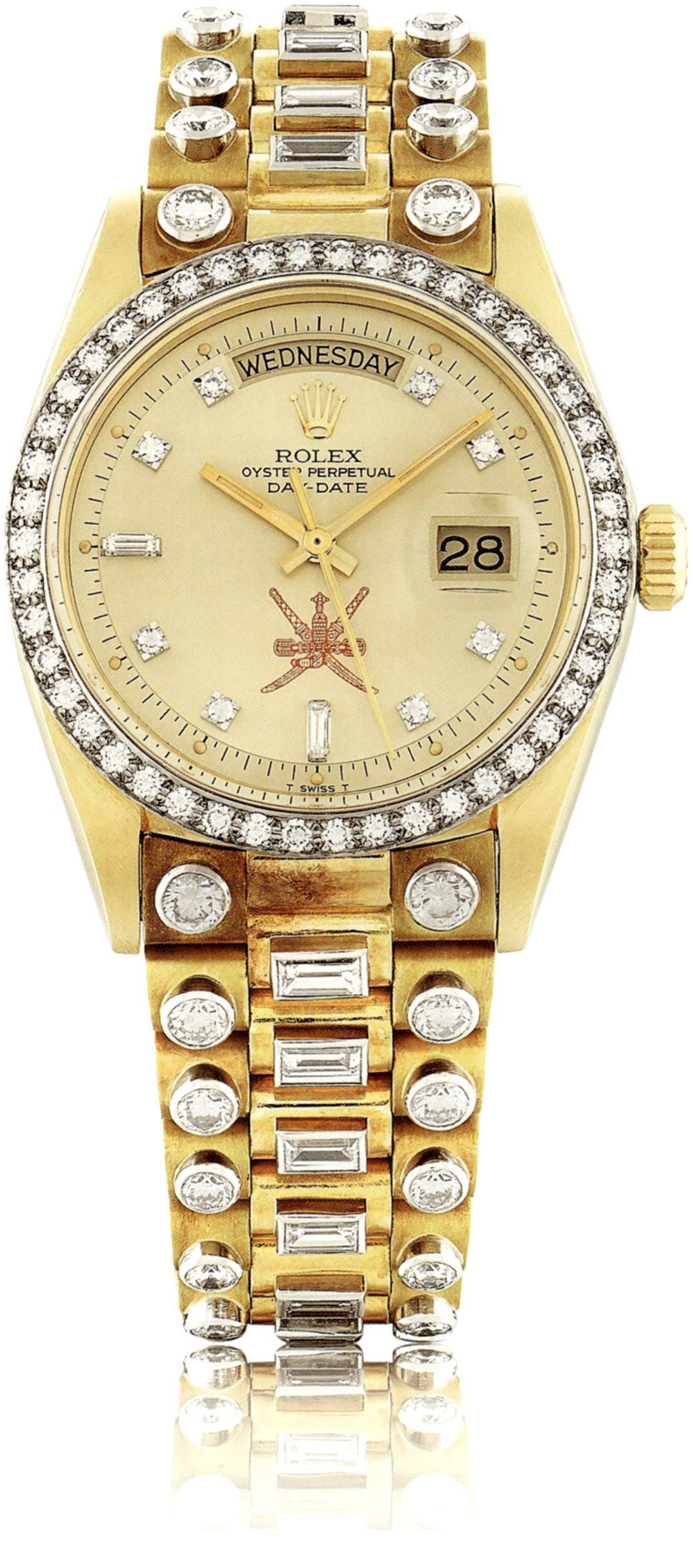

New York, 5 December, 2005

Automatic platinum and diamond wristwatch with day, date and bracelet
Ref. 1802/1804
Oyster Perpetual Day-Date
c.1960

US$ 10,000 – 15,000

SOLD US$ 18,000

The Day-Date was first released in the mid 1950s. It was the first wristwatch to showcase the date and days of the week by two apertures on the dial. Available in different sizes for men and women, there were a number of variations from the basic stainless-steel model to precious metals such as platinum and gold.

Ref. 1802 has a smooth bezel, as opposed to the fluted bezel of Ref. 1803. This makes the 1802 a much rarer and harder to find timepiece.

Geneva, 13 November, 2018

Diamond-set platinum wristwatch
with day and date
Made for the Sultanate of Oman
Ref. 1831
Day-Date 'Khanjar No. 9'
c.1977

CHF 40,000 – 80,000
US$ 40,400 – 81,000

SOLD CHF 65,000

This Rolex Day-Date automatic Ref. 1831 with Khanjar dial and housed within a solid platinum case is one of nine pieces. It bears the emblem of the Sultanate of Oman and may have been gifted in the late '70s by Sultan Qaboos bin Said of Oman to the first Premier of Djibouti upon gaining its independence from France.

New York, 5 December, 2018

Rare automatic diamond-set yellow-gold wristwatch with centre seconds, day, date and diamond-set turquoise laquer dial
Ref. 18108
Day-Date 'Stella'
*c.*1986

US$ 25,000 – 40,000
€ 21,900 – 35,100
HK$ 196,000 – 314,000

NOT SOLD

In 1977 Rolex created the new calibre 3055 and a digit was added to the reference series with the last number indicating the case material; so the 1800 series evolved into the 18000 series.

Reference 18108 appeared for the first time in Rolex's 1978 catalogue, together with references 18026, 18028, 18038, 18039, 18046, 18048, 18049, 18078, 18079, 18168, 18039Bic and 18129Bic.

Geneva, 14 May, 2014

Automatic diamond-set yellow-gold wristwatch with centre seconds, day and date
Ref. 18038
Case 6712986
Day-Date
c.1981

CHF 6,000 – 10,000
US$ 6,900 – 11,400

SOLD CHF 15,000

The reference 18038 was quite a game-changer for the Rolex Day-Date in 1978, the dial lost its pie-pan shape and was the first Day-Date with the 5-digit reference number to receive the sapphire crystal.

The 18000-series watches were in production for 10 years, with the successor introduced in 1988. During the production years of the 18000-series, the weekday indication was available in 25 languages.

1 Geneva, 14 May, 2014

Automatic yellow-gold wristwatch with centre seconds, day, date and opal dial
Ref. 18038/18000
Case 6372076
Day-Date
*c.*1980

CHF 8,000 – 12,000
US$ 9,100 – 13,700

SOLD CHF 16,250

1

2 Geneva, 13 November, 2018

Yellow-gold wristwatch with Stella dial and bracelet
Ref. 18038
Day-Date
*c.*1984

CHF 25,000 – 35,000
US$ 25,300 – 35,300

SOLD CHF 31,250

2

1 Geneva, 12 May, 2019

Diamond-set yellow-gold wristwatch with day, date and apple-green Stella dial
Ref. 18038
Day-Date
c.1988

CHF 30,000 – 40,000
US$ 30,000 – 40,000

SOLD CHF 37,500

2 Geneva, 12 May, 2019

Yellow-gold wristwatch with Arabic day and date, Tiger's-eye hardstone dial and bracelet
Ref. 18038
'Khanjar' Day-Date,
c.1980

CHF 25,000 – 35,000
US$ 25,000 – 35,000

SOLD CHF 35,000

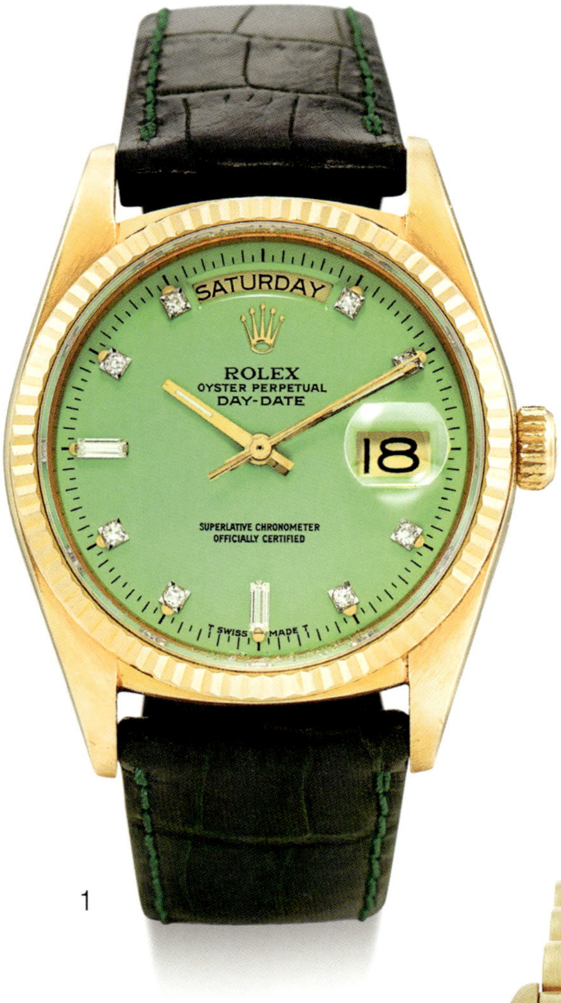

1

2

Geneva, 12 May, 2019

Yellow-gold wristwatch with day, date and walnut-wood dial
Ref. 18038
Day-Date
c.1986

CHF 8,000 – 12,000
US$ 8,000 – 12,000

SOLD CHF 12,500

Geneva, 14 May, 2016

Automatic white-gold wristwatch
with centre seconds, day, date, lapis
lazuli dial and bracelet
Ref. 18039
Case 8031940
Day-Date
c.1985

CHF 28,000 – 48,000
US$ 28,800 – 49,300

SOLD CHF 35,000

Geneva, 15 November, 2016

Automatic diamond-set yellow-gold wristwatch with centre seconds and bracelet; dial set with diamonds, rubies and sapphires
Ref. 18048
Case 8202831
Day-Date
c.1985

CHF 40,000 – 60,000
US$ 41,000 – 61,500

SOLD CHF 75,000

This Day-Date is fitted with a most audacious and eye-catching dial decorated with a honeycomb pattern of alternating rubies and sapphires; the centres of the hexagons are pavé-set with diamonds.

Geneva, 13 May, 2018

Very rare automatic diamond-set yellow-gold wristwatch with day, date and bracelet
Ref. 18048
Case 7347654
Day-Date
*c.*1982

CHF 25,000 – 35,000
US$ 26,000 – 36,400

SOLD CHF 35,000

Reference 18048 is an elegant variant of the Day-Date model adorned with 44 brilliant-cut diamonds along the bezel and diamond hour markers.

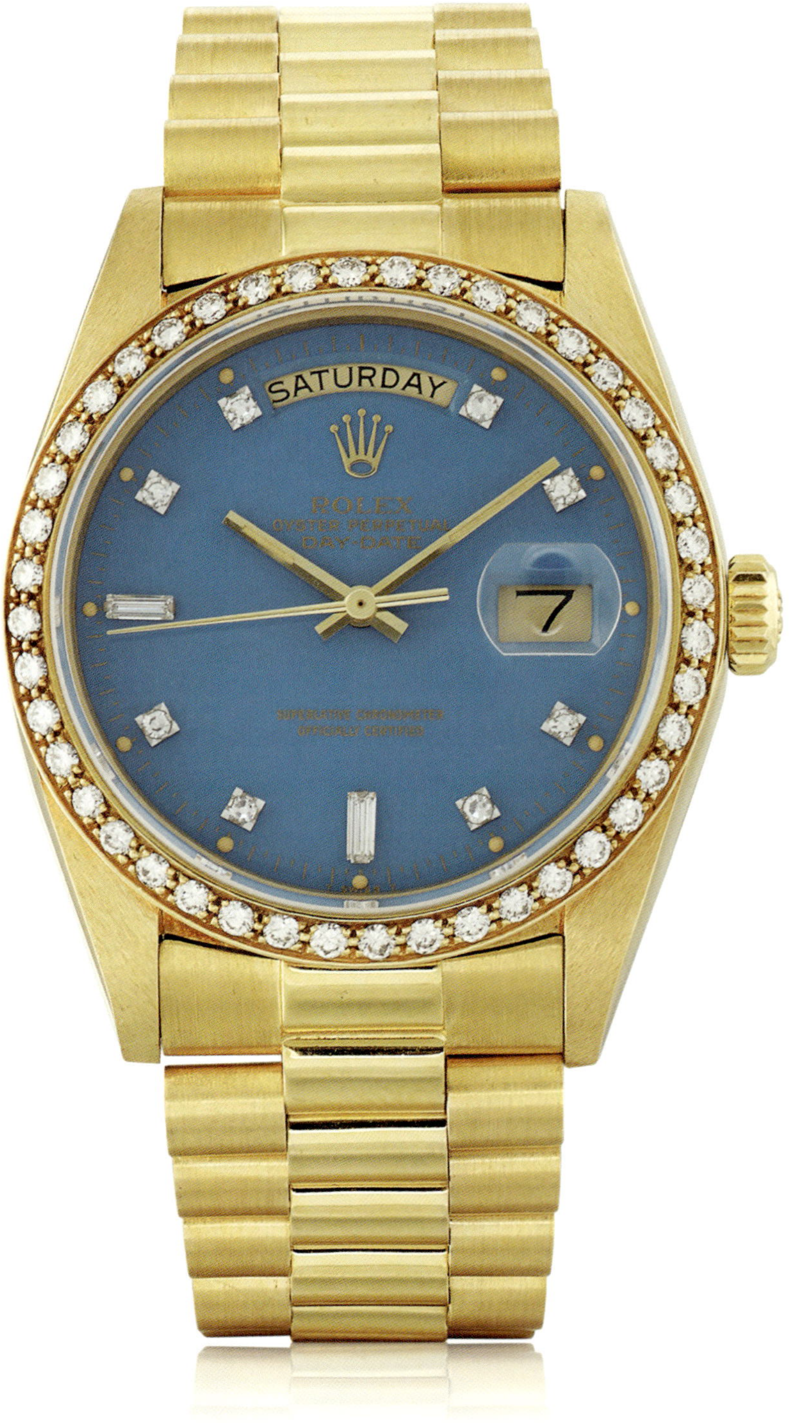

London, 25 September, 2018

Diamond-set yellow-gold wristwatch with centre seconds, day, date and bracelet; diamond-, sapphire- and ruby-set honeycomb dial
Ref. 19048
Case 6744577
Oyster quartz
Day-Date
*c.*1981

£ 20,000 – 40,000
€ 22,400 – 44,800
US$ 26,000 – 52,000

SOLD £ 35,000

This Day-Date Oyster quartz is fitted with one of the rarest, most audacious and eye-catching dials Rolex has ever produced: a honeycomb of alternating rubies and sapphires. The centre of the hexagons are pavé-set with diamonds.

It is interesting to note that this example is only signed 'Rolex Day-Date'; 'Oyster quartz' is not present. This tends to confirm the very limited production of these dials, which were fitted on automatic and quartz Day-Date models. Their scarcity and bold look render pieces bearing these dials treasured by collectors.

Geneva, 12 November, 2013

Automatic yellow-gold wristwatch with centre seconds, day, date and bracelet
Ref. 18238
Case X277927
Day-Date
c.1991

CHF 6,000 – 8,000
US$ 6,500 – 8,700

SOLD CHF 11,250

In 1988, Rolex introduced the new movement, calibre 3155, for the Day-Date generation. This movement – quite an improvement over the 3055 – was the first Rolex movement to have a double quickset function, making it very easy to correct the weekday and date. The movement construction was also changed, with the escapement now attached to a double bridge. This movement was first used in the Rolex Day-Date reference 18200 series.

Geneva, 13 May, 2018

Yellow-gold wristwatch with day, date, lapis lazuli dial and bracelet
Ref. 18238
Day-Date
c.1993

CHF 25,000 – 35,000
US$ 25,300 – 35,300

SOLD CHF 30,000

Geneva, 12 November, 2013

Very rare automatic white-gold wristwatch with centre seconds, day, date and bracelet
Ref. 18239
Case E201227
Day-Date 'Briar root dial'
*c.*1990

CHF 18,000 – 38,000
US$ 25,300 – 35,300

SOLD CHF 30,000

Since 1956, the Oyster Day-Date has been fitted with an aperture showing the days of the week in a choice of 26 different languages. Over the years, the model has been available with a variety of different dial designs, of which this example is one of the rarest. The Day-Date models bear the official wording 'Superlative Chronometer Officially Certified' indicating that the watches were submitted to the Official Swiss Chronometer Control and successfully passed 360 hours of rigorous testing.

Geneva, 12 May, 2019

Diamond-set white-gold wristwatch with day, date and grossular rubellite hardstone dial
Ref. 18249
Day-Date
c.1991

CHF 20,000 – 30,000

SOLD CHF 25,000

Throughout the 1980s and early '90s, Rolex manufactured small quantities of 'special dials', which were offered to retailers without being published in the firm's master catalogue.

The manufacturing process of these natural hardstone dials is extremely difficult. As no two stones are alike, the end result is an exceptional wristwatch with essentially a unique dial.

Geneva, 14 May, 2016

Rare diamond-set yellow-gold wristwatch with centre seconds, day, date and coral dial
Ref. 18388 MVT 6913988
Case S9353575
Day-Date
c.1995

CHF 60,000 – 80,000
US$ 62,000 – 82,500

NOT SOLD

The Day-Date reference 18388 is known for featuring diamonds on its bezel and the four lugs of the case.

Day-Date underwent a 'funky' update in the 1970s, with the release of new highly colourful dials. Coated with a glossy lacquer and boasting a wide range of colours, including pink, orange, pale blue and many more, these watches were initially targeted at the Middle-Eastern buyer, but did not convince the markets at the time. In recent years, collectability of the Stella-dialled Day-Dates has sky-rocketed, with fewer and fewer quality examples available on the market.

New York, 5 December, 2018

Rare automatic diamond-set
yellow-gold wristwatch with centre
seconds, day, date and diamond-set
yellow laquer dial
Ref. 18388
Day-Date 'Taxi Cab Stella'
c.1988

US$ 70,000 – 120,000
€ 61,500 – 106,000
HK$ 550,000 – 945,000

NOT SOLD

London, 25 April, 2017

Automatic diamond-set platinum wristwatch with centre seconds, mother-of-pearl dial, day, date and bracelet
Ref. 18946
Case P198281
Day-Date Masterpiece
*c.*2000

£ 20,000 – 30,000
€ 23,100 – 34,600
US$ 24,500 – 36,700

SOLD £ 30,000

In the early 2000s, Rolex introduced new, special edition Day-Date watches fitted with the Pearlmaster bracelet. These watches were called the Day-Date Masterpiece.

Classic Day-Date cases were 36mm, while the Masterpiece was 39mm in diameter. Moreover, it had a Pearlmaster bracelet rather than the Rolex President bracelet.

A special attribute of the Masterpiece was that they all came adorned with diamonds on the bezel and on the dial.

The Masterpiece series was discontinued in the early 2010s, and it is now one of the most sought-after Day-Date watches in the world.

New York, 4 June, 2019

Automatic platinum wristwatch with centre seconds, day, date and bracelet
Ref. 118206
Day-Date 'Glacier Roman'
c.2014

US$ 20,000 – 30,000
€ 17,700 – 26,600
HK$ 157,000 – 236,000

SOLD US$ 32,500

At Baselworld 2000, Rolex presented the 118000 series with the references 118205, 118206, 118238 and 118239.

ROLEX
QUARTZ

BETA 21

1 Geneva, 14 May, 2014

Rare heavy electronic white-gold wristwatch with date and bracelet
Ref. 5100, No. 758
Beta 21
c.1978

CHF 30,000 – 50,000
US$ 34,100 – 57,000

SOLD CHF 125,000

2 Geneva, 14 May, 2014

Rare heavy electronic yellow-gold wristwatch with date and bracelet
Ref. 5100, No. 590
Case 039
Beta 21
c.1976

CHF 20,000 – 30,000
US$ 22,800 – 34,100

SOLD CHF 87,500

Made in a limited production of only 1,000 examples, the design of Ref. 5100 was completely revolutionary with its angular shaped Oyster case. In recent years these models have become very collectible, due to their rarity and unusual retro styling.

Each Rolex Quartz is engraved with its edition number, seen here are (1) No. 758 and (2) No. 590. The latter was sold by the Rolex agent Artland Watch Co. in Hong Kong, on 19 May 1976.

Geneva, 10 November, 2015

Very rare electronic wristwatch with centre seconds, date and bracelet
Ref. 5100/8 No. 007
MVT 00006990
Beta 21
c.1970

CHF 20,000 – 30,000
US$ 22,800 – 37,100

SOLD CHF 43,750

The Beta 21 movement, released at the Basel fair in April 1970, was the product of nearly 10 years of research and development by C.E.H. (Centre Electronique Hologer), a consortium of Swiss watch firms including Rolex, Patek Philippe, Piaget, I.W.C., Omega and Longines, all of which were interested in developing an electric watch movement. As soon as the Beta 21 calibre was released, Rolex launched this model, Ref. 5100. It was the first Rolex to have a sapphire crystal and the quick date-change mechanism.

Edmond Zaugg was project manager in charge of the development of the electronic calibre within the Rolex manufacture. This watch – presented to Mr. Zaugg to reward him for his brilliant work – is a reference 5100/8, which is extremely rare due to its dark-blue dial, a feature very seldom seen.

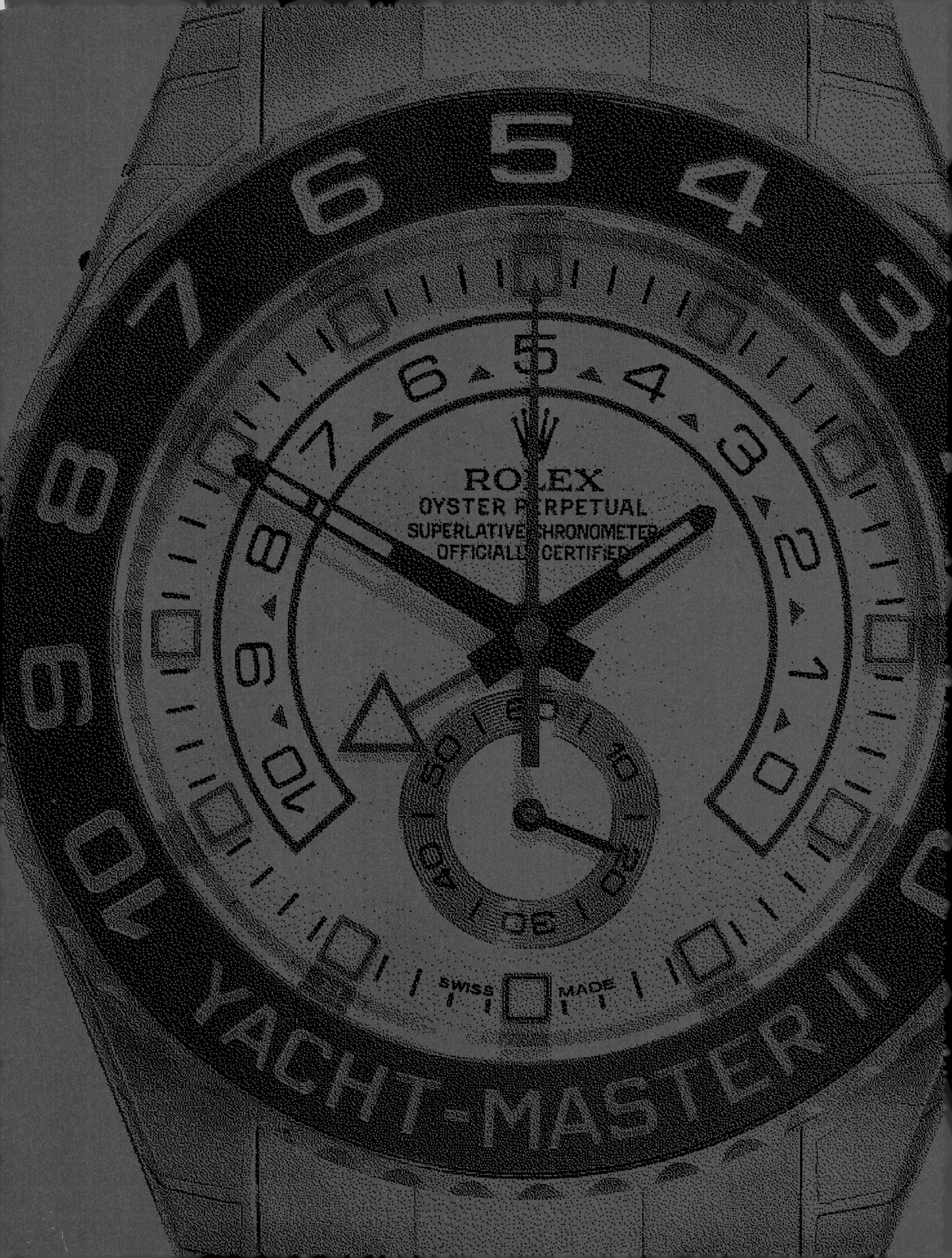
ROLEX
SWISS
MADE
YACHT-MASTER II

YACHT-MASTER II

London, 22 September, 2015

Automatic white-gold chronograph wristwatch with Regatta countdown and bracelet
Ref. 116689
Case Z976346
Yacht-Master II
*c.*2007

£ 8,000 – 12,000
€ 11,400 – 17,100
US$ 12,500 – 18,700

SOLD £ 16,250

Ref. 116689 was introduced in 2007. The Yacht-Master II features the world's first programmable wristwatch with mechanical count-down memory. By rotating the 'command module' bezel, the user can alter the central count-down from 10 minutes to 1 minute as required according to the rules of the regatta in which the wearer is participating.

London, 22 September, 2015

Automatic pink-gold and stainless-steel chronograph wristwatch with Regatta countdown and bracelet
Ref. 116681
Case 2J076740
Yacht-Master II
*c.*2014

£ 6,000 – 9,000
€ 8,600 – 12,900
US$ 9,400 – 14,100

SOLD £ 12,500

The Rolex Yacht-Master II was unveiled in 2007 and first introduced with the references 116688 (yellow gold) and 116689 (white gold). In 2011, Rolex introduced its steel and pink-gold model: Ref. 116681.

Reference	Production started	Production ended	Illustrated

PRINCE

971	1928	1940s	p.22
1490	1928	1940s	pp.22-23
1527	1935	—	p.24
1491	1930	1940s	pp.24-25
2771	1930s	—	p.26

Sporting Prince

1879	1930s	1935	p.27

CHRONOGRAPH

Single-button Chronograph

2022	1929	1935	p.30
2057	1930	—	p.31

Centregraph

3346	1930s	—	p.32

Chronograph

2508	1930s	—	p.33
2917-2918	1930s (mid)	—	p.34
3055	1930s (mid)	—	p.35
3233	1938	1941	p.36
3335	1939	1940	p.37
3484	1937	1948	p.38
3525	1939	1946	pp.39-41
3666	1930s (end)	1940s	p.42
3695	1940	1941	p.43
3835	1940s	—	p.44
4048	1935	1940s	p.45
4500	1940	—	pp.46-47
4062	1942	1963	p.48
8206	1940s (2nd half)	1940s (end)	p.49
6032	1950	1960s (early)	p.50
6034	1950s (1st half)	1950s (mid)	pp.51-52
6234	1955	1961	pp.53-54

'Pre Daytona' Chronograph

6238	1960	1968	pp.55-61

Reference	Production started	Production ended	Illustrated

COSMOGRAPH DAYTONA

6239	1963	1969	pp.64-80, 91, 92, 102, 103
6240	1965	1969	pp.81-82
6241	1965	1969	pp.72, 83-88, 91, 116, 117
6262	1968	1972	pp.69, 89-94, 99, 104, 128
6263	1969	1988	pp.92, 95-115, 122, 125, 127
6264	1969	1972	pp.116-120
6265	1971	1988	pp.121-129
6269	1976	1988	p.130
16519	1988	2000	p.131
16520	1988	2000	p.132
16523	1988	2000	p.133
16528	1989	2000	p.134
116519	2000	2016	p.135
116520	2000	2016	pp.136-137
116589	2000	—	p.138
116598	2004	2019	pp.139-140
116599	2004	—	p.141
116599RBW	2012	—	pp.142-143

OYSTER PERPETUAL

3372	1933	1940s (mid)	pp.146-147
6085	1950s (1st half)	1950s	p.148
6290	1950s (1st half)	1950s	p.149
16013	1977	1980s (mid)	p.150
69028	1980s (2nd half)	—	p.151

DATO COMPAX

4767	1940s (late)	—	pp.154-155
6036	1948	1957	pp.156-158
6236	1958	1962	pp.159-161

MOONPHASE

8171	1949	1952	pp.164-169
6062	1948	1950s (mid)	pp.170-175

ROLEX MODELS – PRODUCTION YEARS

Reference	Production started	Production ended	Illustrated
SUBMARINER			
6200	1954	1956	p.178
6536/1	1956	1959	pp.179-180
6538	1956	1959	pp.181-185
5508	1957	1961	pp.186-187
5510	1958	1958	pp.188-189
5512	1959	1978	pp.190-192
5513	1962	1989	pp.193-199, 200
5514	1970s	—	pp.200-201
5517	1971	1979	pp.202-203
1680	1967	1978	pp.204-206
16800	1978	1987	p.207
16610	1987	2010	p.208
16618	1988	2008	p.209
116610	2010	2020	p.210
166649	2010	—	p.211
TURN-O-GRAPH			
6202	1953	1956	pp.214-217
MILGAUSS			
6541	1954	1962	pp.220-223
1019	1956	1988	pp.224-225
GMT-MASTER			
6542	1954	1959	pp.228-232
1675	1959	1980	pp.233-238
16758	1981	1988	pp.239-240
116758	1981	—	p.241
116759	2007	—	pp.242-243
116749 SABLNR	2017	—	pp.244-245
SEA-DWELLER			
1665	1967	1981	pp.248-255
16600	1989	2009	p.256
16600	?	?	p.257

Reference	Production started	Production ended	Illustrated
EXPLORER			
1016	1960s (early)	1989	pp.260-263
Explorer II			
1655	1971	1985	pp.264-267
16550	1984	1988	pp.268-270
216570	2012	—	pp.271-273
TRU-BEAT			
6556	1954	1959	pp.276-279
DAY-DATE			
1803	1961	1978	pp.282-284
1804	1961	1978	pp.285-288, 289
1802	1963	1978	p.289
1831	1975	1977	p.290
18108	1978	1988	p.291
18038	1978	1988	pp.292-295
18039	1978	1988	p.296
18048	1978	1988	pp.297-298
19048	1978	1988	p.299
18238	1988	2000	pp.300-301
18239	1988	2000	p.302
18249	1988	2000	p.303
18388	1988	2000	pp.304-305
18946	2000s (early)	2010s (early)	p.306
118206	2000	—	p.307
BETA 21			
5100	1970	1972	pp.310-311
YACHT-MASTER II			
116689	2007	—	p.314
116681	2011	—	p.315

	$	HK$	£	€	CHF
1980	1.000	4.779	0.40740	N/A	1.598
1985	1.000	8.580	0.894	N/A	2.651
1990	1.000	7.880	0.622	N/A	1.558
1995	1.000	7.795	0.631	N/A	1.320
2000	1.000	7.810	0.618	N/A	1.591
2005	1.000	7.785	0.516	712	1.233
2010	1.000	7.74550	0.61850	0.69760	1.03570
2015	1.000	7.75510	0.64192	0.82658	0.99431
2020	1.000	7.80825	0.75385	0.89317	0.97079

Goldberger, John, *100 Superlative Rolex Watches*, Damiani Editions, Bologna 2008

Dowling, James M. and Hess, Jeffrey P., *The Best of Time Rolex Watches: An Unauthorized History*, Schiffer Pub Ltd, Atglen (Usa) 2001

Skeet, Martin and Urul Nick, *Vintage Rolex Sports Models: A Complete Visual Reference & Unauthorized History*, Schiffer Pub Ltd, Atglen (Usa) 2005

Gobbi, Paolo, *Cronografi Rolex - La Leggenda*, Pucci Papaleo Editore, Rome 2005

Pergola, Carlo, Mazzariol, Stefano and Dosso, Giovanni, *Rolex Daytona a legend is born*, Vintage Watches, Prato 2005

Patrizzi, Osvaldo, *Collecting Rolex Wristwatches*, Mondani Editore, Milano 2001

Patrizzi Osvaldo, *Cosmograph Daytona Manual Winding*, Action Group Editore, Milano 2010

Patrizzi, Osvaldo and Cappelletti, Mara, *Rolex - History, icons and record-breaking models*, ACC, London 2015

ISBN: 978-178884-124-5

British Library Cataloguing-in-Publication Data
A catalogue record for this book is available from the British Library

The authors and publisher gratefully acknowledge the permission granted to reproduce the copyright material in this book. Every effort has been made to trace copyright holders and to obtain their permission for the use of copyright material. The publisher apologises for any errors or omissions in the text and would be grateful if notified of any corrections that should be incorporated in future reprints or editions of this book.

Editor's and Authors' Notes
The source for all data contained in this book is Sotheby's.
Catalogues have been written in different years, in different countries and by different people, it is thus normal to find differences in style and format.

The dates published in the book refer to the information known at the time of the various catalogues as published by Sotheby's. Production dates refer to mainstream reference production periods.
Caption dates refer to the year of sale as per Sotheby's records. Sale dates refer to the year a specific model was sold and this may have taken place slightly earlier or later than production dates.

All prices are as at time of sale and include sales commission.
For prices update please refer to the currency converter table on page 318.

FSC www.fsc.org MIX Paper from responsible sources FSC® C106600

Printed in Slovenia
for ACC Art Books Ltd., Woodbridge, Suffolk, UK

www.accartbooks.com

ACC ART BOOKS

Frontispiece:
Cosmograph Daytona 'Paul Newman', Ref. 6239, see p.69

Front cover:
Left: Yacht-Master II, Ref. 116689, see p.314
Centre: Cosmograph Daytona 'Paul Newman', Ref 6239, see p.75 (top)
Right: Explorer II, Ref 16550, see p.268

Back cover:
Top: Sea-Dweller 'Double Red', Ref. 1665, see p.255
Bottom: GMT-Master II, Ref. 116749 SABLNR, see p.244